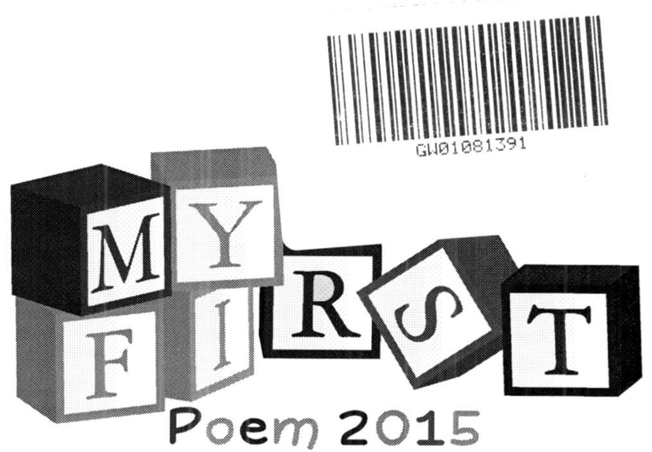


# Around The UK

Edited by Jenni Bannister

First published in Great Britain in 2015 by:

Remus House
Coltsfoot Drive
Peterborough
PE2 9BF
Telephone: 01733 890066
Website: www.youngwriters.co.uk


Book Design by Spencer Hart

SB ISBN 978-1-78443-711-4

Printed and bound in the UK by BookPrintingUK
Website: www.bookprintinguk.com

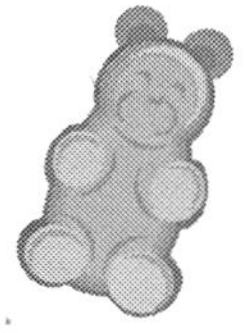

# Foreword

Dear Reader,

Young Writers was established in 1991 with the aim of encouraging writing skills in young people and giving them the opportunity to see their work in print. Poetry is a wonderful way to introduce young children to the idea of rhyme and rhythm and helps learning and development of communication, language and literacy skills.

'My First Poem' was created to introduce nursery and preschool children to this wonderful world of poetry. They were given a template to fill in with their own words, creating a poem that was all about them.

We are proud to present the resulting collection of personal and touching poems in this anthology, which can be treasured for years to come.

Jenni Bannister

Editorial Manager

# Contents

## Child's Play Preschool, Banbridge



## Dervock Community Playgroup, Ballymoney



## Happy Tots Playgroup, Lisburn



## Hillcrest Day Nursery, Belfast



## Hillside Preschool, Guernsey



## Little Friends Playgroup, Omagh

## Little Friends Preschool, Banbridge



## Little Rays Day Nursery, Ballymena



## Little Wombles Cross-Community Playgroup, Magherafelt



## Maylands Nursery, St Saviours



## Mother Goose Playgroup, Ballycastle



## Preschool Duval, Guernsey

## St Joseph's Community Playgroup, Londonderry



## St Mary's Preschool Centre, Strabane



## St Paul's Nursery School, Belfast



## The Beeches Day Nursery, Craigavon



## The Country Preschool, Ballymena

## The Old School House, Lisburn



## Willaston Playgroup, Isle Of Man

# The Poems

# My First Poem

My name is Lily and I go to preschool,
My best friend is Alexis, who is really cool.
I watch Bob the Builder on TV,
Playing with cars is lots of fun for me.
I just love Cornflakes to eat,
And sometimes chocolate cake for a treat.
Pink is a colour I like a lot,
My dino is the best present I ever got.
My favourite person is Lily, who is a gem,
So this, my first poem, is just for them!

Lily Jensen

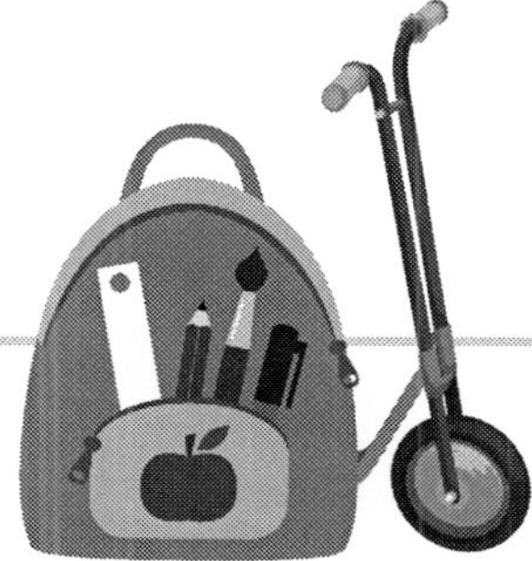

# My First Poem

My name is Demi and I go to preschool,
My best friend is Jessica, who is really cool.
I watch cartoons on TV,
Playing mums and dads is lots of fun for me.
I just love potatoes to eat,
And sometimes sweets for a treat.
Red is a colour I like a lot,
My Minnie Mouse is the best present I ever got.
My favourite person is my sister, who is a gem,
So this, my first poem, is just for them!

Demi Stanley (3)

# My First Poem

My name is Mina and I go to preschool,
My best friend is Elisa, who is really cool.
I watch Frozen on TV,
Playing with Peppa Pig toys is lots of fun for me.
I just love apples to eat,
And sometimes sweets for a treat.
Pink is a colour I like a lot,
My Peppa Pig toy is the best present I ever got.
My favourite person is Mummy, who is a gem,
So this, my first poem, is just for them!

Mina Moharrem

# My First Poem

My name is Ella and I go to preschool,
My best friend is Phoebe, who is really cool.
I watch SpongeBob on TV,
Playing outside is lots of fun for me.
I just love carrots to eat,
And sometimes sweeties and chocolate for a treat.
Pink is a colour I like a lot,
My Ariel toy is the best present I ever got.
My favourite person is Alfie, who is a gem,
So this, my first poem, is just for them!

Ella Maylor (4)

# My First Poem

My name is Fionnian and I go to preschool,
My best friend is Harry, who is really cool.
I watch Teenage Mutant Ninja Turtles on TV,
Playing with my Turtles is lots of fun for me.
I just love chicken nuggets to eat,
And sometimes chocolate eggs for a treat.
Blue is a colour I like a lot,
My Turtle is the best present I ever got.
My favourite person is my mummy, who is a gem,
So this, my first poem, is just for them!

Fionnian McDonald (3)
Ashgrove Preschool Playgroup, Craigavon

# My First Poem

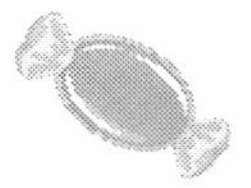

My name is Ella-Rose and I go to preschool,
My best friend is Bella, who is really cool.
I watch Frozen on TV,
Playing on my horse is lots of fun for me.
I just love chips to eat,
And sometimes biccies for a treat.
Pink is a colour I like a lot,
My Elsa make-up is the best present I ever got.
My favourite person is my mummy, who is a gem,
So this, my first poem, is just for them!

Ella-Rose Sands (3)
Ashgrove Preschool Playgroup, Craigavon

# My First Poem

My name is Aiden and I go to preschool,
My best friend is Fionnian, who is really cool.
I watch Fireman Sam on TV,
Playing with my blocks is lots of fun for me.
I just love porridge and sugar to eat,
And sometimes sweets for a treat.
Green is a colour I like a lot,
My go-kart is the best present I ever got.
My favourite person is my mummy, who is a gem,
So this, my first poem, is just for them!

Aiden Livingston (3)
Ashgrove Preschool Playgroup, Craigavon

# My First Poem

My name is Caellum and I go to preschool,
My best friend is my sister, who is really cool.
I watch Mickey Mouse Clubhouse on TV,
Playing with my cars is lots of fun for me.
I just love pasta to eat,
And sometimes a wee sweetie for a treat.
Green is a colour I like a lot,
My bike is the best present I ever got.
My favourite person is my mummy, who is a gem,
So this, my first poem, is just for them!

Caellum Hendron (3)
Ashgrove Preschool Playgroup, Craigavon

# My First Poem

My name is Maisie and I go to preschool,
My best friend is Bella, who is really cool.
I watch Peppa Pig on TV,
Playing with my vampire dog is lots of fun for me.
I just love McDonald's chips and burger to eat,
And sometimes jelly babies for a treat.
Pink is a colour I like a lot,
My doll is the best present I ever got.
My favourite person is Sparky the dog, who is a gem,
So this, my first poem, is just for them!

Maisie Halfpenny (3)
Ashgrove Preschool Playgroup, Craigavon

# My First Poem

My name is Cadhla and I go to preschool,
My best friend is Hallie, who is really cool.
I watch Frozen on TV,
Playing with my Frozen dolls is lots of fun for me.
I just love spaghetti Bolognese to eat,
And sometimes sweeties for a treat.
Pink is a colour I like a lot,
My doll is the best present I ever got.
My favourite person is my mummy, who is a gem,
So this, my first poem, is just for them!

Cadhla Hughes (3)
Ashgrove Preschool Playgroup, Craigavon

# My First Poem

My name is Dyanté-Logan and I go to preschool,
My best friend is Reece, who is really cool.
I watch Garfield on TV,
Playing in my cars is lots of fun for me.
I just love ice cream to eat,
And sometimes makes my dream for a treat.
Blue is a colour I like a lot,
My DS is the best present I ever got.
My favourite person is Mum, who is a gem,
So this, my first poem, is just for them!

Dyanté-Logan Duffey (4)
Aughnacloy Playgroup Ltd, Aughnacloy

# My First Poem

My name is Sarah-Jane and I go to preschool,
My best friend is Laura, who is really cool.
I watch Peppa Pig on TV,
Playing with jigsaws is lots of fun for me.
I just love apples, oranges and plums to eat,
And sometimes a Mars bar for a treat.
Purple is a colour I like a lot,
My pink bike is the best present I ever got.
My favourite person is Dada, who is a gem,
So this, my first poem, is just for them!

Sarah-Jane Boyd (3)
Aughnacloy Playgroup Ltd, Aughnacloy

# My First Poem

My name is Robbie and I go to preschool,
My best friend is Isaac, who is really cool.
I watch Buzz and Woody from Toy Story on TV,
Playing Spider-Man is lots of fun for me.
I just love cereal to eat,
And sometimes chocolate buns for a treat.
Blue is a colour I like a lot,
My Buzz is the best present I ever got.
My favourite person is Mummy, who is a gem,
So this, my first poem, is just for them!

Robbie Herron (3)
Aughnacloy Playgroup Ltd, Aughnacloy

# My First Poem

My name is Jack and I go to preschool,
My best friend is Aaron, who is really cool.
I watch Mister Maker on TV,
Playing farms is lots of fun for me.
I just love broccoli to eat,
And sometimes cabbage for a treat.
Green is a colour I like a lot,
My tractor is the best present I ever got.
My favourite person is Mum, who is a gem,
So this, my first poem, is just for them!

Jack Stinson (4)
Aughnacloy Playgroup Ltd, Aughnacloy

# My First Poem

My name is Caoimhe and I go to preschool,
My best friend is Kayla, who is really cool.
I watch Peter Rabbit on TV,
Playing with Aoibheann and Enda is lots of fun for me.
I just love noodles to eat,
And sometimes ice cream and jelly for a treat.
Pink is a colour I like a lot,
My bike is the best present I ever got.
My favourite person is my daddy, who is a gem,
So this, my first poem, is just for them!

Caoimhe McNamee (3)
Aughnacloy Playgroup Ltd, Aughnacloy

# My First Poem

My name is Jamie and I go to preschool,
My best friend is Jake, who is really cool.
I watch Tractor Ted on TV,
Playing with blocks and outside is lots of fun for me.
I just love salad to eat,
And sometimes chocolate for a treat.
Yellow is a colour I like a lot,
My big tractor and loader is the best present I ever got.
My favourite person is my daddy, who is a gem,
So this, my first poem, is just for them!

Jamie Bell (4)
Aughnacloy Playgroup Ltd, Aughnacloy

# My First Poem

My name is Kayliah and I go to preschool,
My best friend is Caoimhe, who is really cool.
I watch Sofia the First on TV,
Playing with Play-Doh is lots of fun for me.
I just love sausages and chips to eat,
And sometimes chocolate for a treat.
Pink is a colour I like a lot,
My electric Mini Cooper is the best present I ever got.
My favourite person is Daddy, who is a gem,
So this, my first poem, is just for them!

Kayliah Tracey (4)
Aughnacloy Playgroup Ltd, Aughnacloy

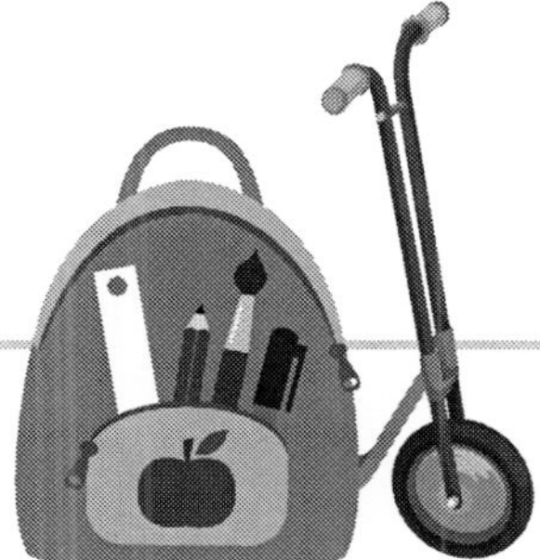

# My First Poem

My name is Áine and I go to preschool,
My best friend is Erin, who is really cool.
I watch CBeebies on TV,
Playing with play dough is lots of fun for me.
I just love ham sandwiches to eat,
And sometimes sweeties for a treat.
Pink is a colour I like a lot,
My Frozen dress is the best present I ever got.
My favourite person is Mummy, who is a gem,
So this, my first poem, is just for them!

Áine Gildernew (4)
Aughnacloy Playgroup Ltd, Aughnacloy

# My First Poem

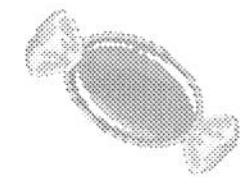

My name is Andrea and I go to preschool,
My best friend is Daniel, who is really cool.
I watch Barbie Princess, Snow White and Cinderella on TV,
Playing music is lots of fun for me.
I just love sausages, chips and sweetcorn to eat,
And sometimes ice cream for a treat.
Pink is a colour I like a lot,
My purple quad is the best present I ever got.
My favourite person is Alannah, my sister, who is a gem,
So this, my first poem, is just for them!

Andrea Eloise Agnew (4)
Aughnacloy Playgroup Ltd, Aughnacloy

# My First Poem

My name is Conan and I go to preschool,
My best friend is Dan, who is really cool.
I watch Tom and Jerry on TV,
Playing Hulk in my toy room is lots of fun for me.
I just love sausages to eat,
And sometimes chocolate bars for a treat.
Blue is a colour I like a lot,
My Power Ranger is the best present I ever got.
My favourite person is Grandad Phil, who is a gem,
So this, my first poem, is just for them!

Conan McGuckin (4)
Ballinderry Playgroup, Cookstown

# My First Poem

My name is Cadan and I go to preschool,
My best friend is Dan, who is really cool.
I watch George the monkey on TV,
Playing with my tractors is lots of fun for me.
I just love potatoes and sweetcorn to eat,
And sometimes sweets for a treat.
Blue is a colour I like a lot,
My tractor is the best present I ever got.
My favourite person is my mummy, who is a gem,
So this, my first poem, is just for them!

Cadan Scullion (4)
Ballinderry Playgroup, Cookstown

# My First Poem

My name is Phillip and I go to preschool,
My best friend is Dylan, who is really cool.
I watch superheroes on TV,
Playing animals is lots of fun for me.
I just love crisp sandwiches to eat,
And sometimes candy sticks for a treat.
Yellow is a colour I like a lot,
My Grimlock is the best present I ever got.
My favourite person is Mum, who is a gem,
So this, my first poem, is just for them!

Phillip Conway (4)
Ballinderry Playgroup, Cookstown

# My First Poem

My name is Zack and I go to preschool,
My best friend is Luke, who is really cool.
I watch Adventure Time on TV,
Playing with my trucks is lots of fun for me.
I just love bread and butter to eat,
And sometimes get sweets for a treat.
Blue is a colour I like a lot,
My battery John Deere is the best present I ever got.
My favourite person is Jay, who is a gem,
So this, my first poem, is just for them!

Zack O'Neill (4)
Ballinderry Playgroup, Cookstown

# My First Poem

My name is Caoimhe and I go to preschool,
My best friend is Buddy the dog, who is really cool.
I watch Scooby-Doo on TV,
Playing hide-and-seek is lots of fun for me.
I just love sausages to eat,
And sometimes marshmallows for a treat.
Blue is a colour I like a lot,
My doll's house is the best present I ever got.
My favourite person is Granny, who is a gem,
So this, my first poem, is just for them!

Caoimhe Harney (4)
Ballinderry Playgroup, Cookstown

# My First Poem

My name is Amy and I go to preschool,
My best friend is Molly, who is really cool.
I watch Minnie Mouse on TV,
Playing with dolls is lots of fun for me.
I just love pancakes to eat,
And sometimes sweets for a treat.
Pink is a colour I like a lot,
My cat is the best present I ever got.
My favourite person is Mummy, who is a gem,
So this, my first poem, is just for them!

Amy Hamilton (4)
Ballinderry Playgroup, Cookstown

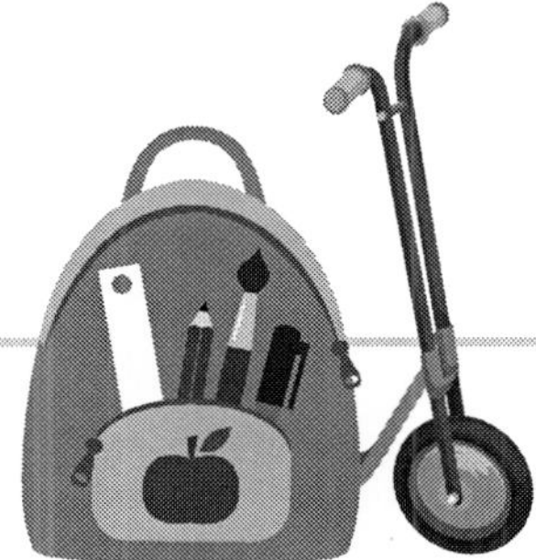

# My First Poem

My name is Shauna and I go to preschool,
My best friend is Molly, who is really cool.
I watch Peppa Pig, Bing and Everything's Rosie on TV,
Playing princesses and fairies is lots of fun for me.
I just love oranges, grapes, pears, apples and strawberries to eat,
And sometimes sweets for a treat.
Pink is a colour I like a lot,
My bicycle is the best present I ever got.
My favourite person is Mummy, who is a gem,
So this, my first poem, is just for them!

Shauna McGuckin (4)
Ballinderry Playgroup, Cookstown

# My First Poem

My name is Isla and I go to preschool,
My best friend is Molly, who is really cool.
I watch Minnie Mouse on TV,
Playing hairdressers is lots of fun for me.
I just love bananas to eat,
And sometimes sweets for a treat.
Pink is a colour I like a lot,
My Frozen bike is the best present I ever got.
My favourite person is my mummy, who is a gem,
So this, my first poem, is just for them!

Isla Conway (4)
Ballinderry Playgroup, Cookstown

# My First Poem

My name is Tiarnán and I go to preschool,
My best friend is Thomas, who is really cool.
I watch Mouseketeers on TV,
Playing superheroes is lots of fun for me.
I just love pancakes to eat,
And sometimes I get sweets for a treat.
Green is a colour I like a lot,
My Spider-Man bike is the best present I ever got.
My favourite person is Mummy, who is a gem,
So this, my first poem, is just for them!

Tíarnán Bell (4)
Ballinderry Playgroup, Cookstown

# My First Poem

My name is Cara Rose and I go to preschool,
My best friend is Emily, who is really cool.
I watch Scooby-Doo on TV,
Playing with Play-Doh is lots of fun for me.
I just love beetroot to eat,
And sometimes chocolate buttons for a treat.
Orange is a colour I like a lot,
My Jeep is the best present I ever got.
My favourite person is Rosie, who is a gem,
So this, my first poem, is just for them!

Cara Rose Mullan (3)
Ballinderry Playgroup, Cookstown

# My First Poem

My name is Ellie and I go to preschool,
My best friend is Shauna, who is really cool.
I watch Ben and Holly's Little Kingdom on TV,
Playing hide-and-seek is lots of fun for me.
I just love burgers and chips to eat,
And sometimes I like chocolate for a treat.
Pink is a colour I like a lot,
My Doc McStuffins mobile clinic is the best present I ever got.
My favourite person is Mummy, who is a gem,
So this, my first poem, is just for them!

Ellie Kathryn Gilligan
Ballinderry Playgroup, Cookstown

# My First Poem

My name is Ryan and I go to preschool,
My best friend is Zack, who is really cool.
I watch Curious George on TV,
Playing outside on my tractor is lots of fun for me.
I just love sausages, potatoes and beans to eat,
And sometimes sweets for a treat.
Blue is a colour I like a lot,
My New Holland tractor is the best present I ever got.
My favourite person is Daddy, who is a gem,
So this, my first poem, is just for them!

Ryan Francis Hamilton (4)
Ballinderry Playgroup, Cookstown

# My First Poem

My name is Lara and I go to preschool,
My best friend is Molly, who is really cool.
I watch The Next Step on TV,
Playing hide-and-seek is lots of fun for me.
I just love corn on the cob to eat,
And sometimes a slush for a treat.
Gold is a colour I like a lot,
My dog, Bailey, is the best present I ever got.
My favourite person is Mummy, who is a gem,
So this, my first poem, is just for them!

Lara McGuckin (4)
Ballinderry Playgroup, Cookstown

# My First Poem

My name is Amy and I go to preschool,
My best friend is Daniel, who is really cool.
I watch Doc McStuffins on TV,
Playing hide-and-seek is lots of fun for me.
I just love cheese and ham sandwiches to eat,
And sometimes chocolate for a treat.
Pink is a colour I like a lot,
My baby doll is the best present I ever got.
My favourite person is Macey, who is a gem,
So this, my first poem, is just for them!

Amy O'Neill (4)
Ballinderry Playgroup, Cookstown

# My First Poem

My name is Dylan and I go to preschool,
My best friend is Phillip, who is really cool.
I watch The Avengers on TV,
Playing superheroes is lots of fun for me.
I just love sweetcorn to eat,
And sometimes Kinder eggs for a treat.
Blue is a colour I like a lot,
My superhero costume is the best present I ever got.
My favourite person is Granny Clare, who is a gem,
So this, my first poem, is just for them!

Dylan Campbell (4)
Ballinderry Playgroup, Cookstown

# My First Poem

My name is Cole and I go to preschool,
My best friend is Conan, who is really cool.
I watch Disney's Cars on TV,
Playing football is lots of fun for me.
I just love chicken nuggets and chips to eat,
And sometimes ice cream for a treat.
Orange is a colour I like a lot,
My bike is the best present I ever got.
My favourite person is Mummy, who is a gem,
So this, my first poem, is just for them!

Cole Nelson (4)
Ballinderry Playgroup, Cookstown

# My First Poem

My name is Oisin and I go to preschool,
My best friend is Conan, who is really cool.
I watch Baby Looney Tunes on TV,
Playing on my DS is lots of fun for me.
I just love pancakes to eat,
And sometimes Smarties for a treat.
Blue is a colour I like a lot,
My DS is the best present I ever got.
My favourite person is Captain America, who is a gem,
So this, my first poem, is just for them!

Oisin Charles Quinn (3)
Ballinderry Playgroup, Cookstown

# My First Poem

My name is Grace and I go to preschool,
My best friend is Philip, who is really cool.
I watch Peppa Pig on TV,
Playing mummies and daddies is lots of fun for me.
I just love spaghetti to eat,
And sometimes a chocolate bar for a treat.
Orange is a colour I like a lot,
My Doc McStuffins check-up centre is the best present I ever got.
My favourite person is Mummy, who is a gem,
So this, my first poem, is just for them!

Grace McVey (4)
Ballinderry Playgroup, Cookstown

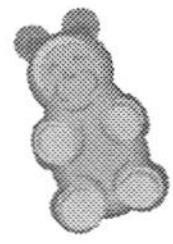

# My First Poem

My name is Brandon and I go to preschool,
My best friend is Tommy, who is really cool.
I watch Tiny Pop on TV,
Playing on my tractor outside is lots of fun for me.
I just love chicken and chips to eat,
And sometimes butterfly sweets for a treat.
Blue is a colour I like a lot,
My toothless teddy is the best present I ever got.
My favourite person is Granny, who is a gem,
So this, my first poem, is just for them!

Brandon Berryman (4)
Ballinderry Playgroup, Cookstown

# My First Poem

My name is Dan and I go to preschool,
My best friend is Kade, who is really cool.
I watch Curious George on TV,
Playing tig is lots of fun for me.
I just love raisins to eat,
And sometimes a Galaxy bar for a treat.
Blue is a colour I like a lot,
My Chelsea jersey is the best present I ever got.
My favourite person is Mummy, who is a gem,
So this, my first poem, is just for them!

Dan Conlan (4)
Ballinderry Playgroup, Cookstown

# My First Poem

My name is Cole and I go to preschool,
My best friend is Lucas, who is really cool.
I watch Alvin and the Chipmunk on TV,
Playing outside is lots of fun for me.
I just love pizza and pasta to eat,
And sometimes sweets for a treat.
Red is a colour I like a lot,
My Spider-Man motorbike is the best present I ever got.
My favourite person is Daddy, who is a gem,
So this, my first poem, is just for them!

Cole Howarth (3)
Barugh Green Preschool, Barnsley

# My First Poem

My name is Sasha and I go to preschool,
My best friend is Cole, who is really cool.
I watch Rango on TV,
Playing on my space hopper is lots of fun for me.
I just love sandwiches to eat,
And sometimes chocolate for a treat.
Green is a colour I like a lot,
My Baby Born is the best present I ever got.
My favourite person is Daddy, who is a gem,
So this, my first poem, is just for them!

Sasha West (3)
Barugh Green Preschool, Barnsley

# My First Poem

My name is Grace and I go to preschool,
My best friend is Phoebe, my sister, who is really cool.
I watch Peppa Pig and Dora on TV,
Playing with my Play-Doh and Lego is lots of fun for me.
I just love pitta bread and pasta to eat,
And sometimes biscuits for a treat.
Pink is a colour I like a lot,
My Y-Fliker is the best present I ever got.
My favourite person is Phoebe, my sister, who is a gem,
So this, my first poem, is just for them!

Grace Lovett (4)
Barugh Green Preschool, Barnsley

# My First Poem

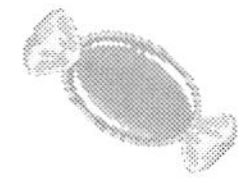

My name is Amy and I go to preschool,
My best friend is Ruby, who is really cool.
I watch Peppa Pig and Sofia the First on TV,
Playing with my big sister is lots of fun for me.
I just love chicken nuggets and porridge to eat,
And sometimes sweets for a treat.
Pink is a colour I like a lot,
My mermaid doll is the best present I ever got.
My favourite person is Mummy, who is a gem,
So this, my first poem, is just for them!

Amy White (3)
Barugh Green Preschool, Barnsley

# My First Poem

My name is Oliver and I go to preschool,
My best friend is Harry, who is really cool.
I watch Peppa Pig on TV,
Playing football is lots of fun for me.
I just love fish and chips to eat,
And sometimes chocolate for a treat.
Blue is a colour I like a lot,
My tree house is the best present I ever got.
My favourite person is Mummy, who is a gem,
So this, my first poem, is just for them!

Oliver O'Mara (4)
Barugh Green Preschool, Barnsley

# My First Poem

My name is Jenson and I go to preschool,
My best friend is Cole, who is really cool.
I watch Peppa Pig on TV,
Playing with Lego is lots of fun for me.
I just love fish and chips to eat,
And sometimes chocolate ice cream for a treat.
Pink is a colour I like a lot,
My Batman house is the best present I ever got.
My favourite person is Maddison, who is a gem,
So this, my first poem, is just for them!

Jenson Lucas Peel (4)
Barugh Green Preschool, Barnsley

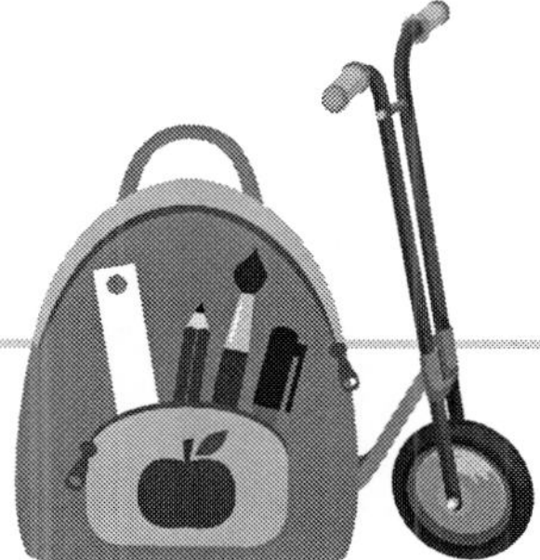

# My First Poem

My name is Olivia and I go to preschool,
My best friend is Maisie, who is really cool.
I watch Ben and Holly on TV,
Playing with jigsaw puzzles is lots of fun for me.
I just love spaghetti Bolognese to eat,
And sometimes chocolate for a treat.
Pink is a colour I like a lot,
My Anna dress is the best present I ever got.
My favourite person is Mummy, who is a gem,
So this, my first poem, is just for them!

Olivia Royce (3)
Barugh Green Preschool, Barnsley

# My First Poem

My name is Eleanor and I go to preschool,
My best friend is Maisie, who is really cool.
I watch Shaun the Sheep on TV,
Playing shopping is lots of fun for me.
I just love porridge to eat,
And sometimes jelly for a treat.
Purple is a colour I like a lot,
My Frozen doll is the best present I ever got.
My favourite person is Poppy, the cat, who is a gem,
So this, my first poem, is just for them!

Eleanor Garner (4)
Barugh Green Preschool, Barnsley

# My First Poem

My name is Freya and I go to preschool,
My best friend is Olivia, who is really cool.
I watch Frozen on TV,
Playing on the slide is lots of fun for me.
I just love Dairylea Dunkers to eat,
And sometimes chocolate for a treat.
Green is a colour I like a lot,
My ballet dress is the best present I ever got.
My favourite person is Isabelle, who is a gem,
So this, my first poem, is just for them!

Freya Bamforth (3)
Barugh Green Preschool, Barnsley

# My First Poem

My name is Robyn and I go to preschool,
My best friend is Ava, who is really cool.
I watch Gigglebiz and Peter Rabbit on TV,
Playing dressing up as princesses is lots of fun for me.
I just love spaghetti and strawberries to eat,
And sometimes chocolate for a treat.
Purple is a colour I like a lot,
My play kitchen is the best present I ever got.
My favourite person is my mummy, who is a gem,
So this, my first poem, is just for them!

Robyn Green (3)
Barugh Green Preschool, Barnsley

# My First Poem

My name is Finlay and I go to preschool,
My best friend is Didi, who is really cool.
I watch Fireman Sam on TV,
Playing with my garage is lots of fun for me.
I just love pasta to eat,
And sometimes chocolate buttons for a treat.
Yellow is a colour I like a lot,
My fire engine is the best present I ever got.
My favourite person is Mummy, who is a gem,
So this, my first poem, is just for them!

Finlay Joseph Falkingham (2)
Barugh Green Preschool, Barnsley

# My First Poem

My name is Elizabeth and I go to preschool,
My best friend is Didi, who is really cool.
I watch The Wiggles on TV,
Playing with my jigsaws is lots of fun for me.
I just love pasta to eat,
And sometimes I like biscuits for a treat.
Red is a colour I like a lot,
My baby Poppy is the best present I ever got.
My favourite person is me, who is a gem,
So this, my first poem, is just for them!

Elizabeth Elsie Falkingham (2)
Barugh Green Preschool, Barnsley

# My First Poem

My name is John and I go to preschool,
My best friend is Lisa, who is really cool.
I watch Scooby-Doo on TV,
Playing football is lots of fun for me.
I just love pizza to eat,
And sometimes chocolate for a treat.
Green is a colour I like a lot,
My football is the best present I ever got.
My favourite person is Daddy, who is a gem,
So this, my first poem, is just for them!

John Jacob Conway (3)
Barugh Green Preschool, Barnsley

# My First Poem

My name is Jessica and I go to preschool,
My best friend is Maisie, who is really cool.
I watch Sofia on TV,
Playing games is lots of fun for me.
I just love pasta to eat,
And sometimes the seaside for a treat.
Silver is a colour I like a lot,
My Elsa doll is the best present I ever got.
My favourite person is my mummy, who is a gem,
So this, my first poem, is just for them!

Jessica Holmes (3)
Barugh Green Preschool, Barnsley

# My First Poem

My name is Mason and I go to preschool,
My best friend is Jenson, who is really cool.
I watch Fireman Sam on TV,
Playing in the garden is lots of fun for me.
I just love noodles and scrambled eggs to eat,
And sometimes ice cream for a treat.
Blue is a colour I like a lot,
My battery operated car, a red Audi is the best present I ever got.
My favourite person is my mum, who is a gem,
So this, my first poem, is just for them!

Mason Roberts-Morgan (2)
Barugh Green Preschool, Barnsley

# My First Poem

My name is Zak and I go to preschool,
My best friend is Lucy, who is really cool.
I watch Mr Tumble on TV,
Playing with tools fixing and building is lots of fun for me.
I just love sausages to eat,
And sometimes biscuits for a treat.
Blue is a colour I like a lot,
My tool set is the best present I ever got.
My favourite person is Mason, who is a gem,
So this, my first poem, is just for them!

Zak Jordan Mills
Barugh Green Preschool, Barnsley

# My First Poem

My name is Oscar and I go to preschool,
My best friend is Isaac, who is really cool.
I watch Aquabats on TV,
Playing with cars is lots of fun for me.
I just love sauce to eat,
And sometimes Crunchies for a treat.
Yellow is a colour I like a lot,
My red robot is the best present I ever got.
My favourite person is Freddie, who is a gem,
So this, my first poem, is just for them!

Oscar Wajner (3)
Barugh Green Preschool, Barnsley

# My First Poem

My name is Alyssa and I go to preschool,
My best friend is Ava, who is really cool.
I watch Peppa Pig on TV,
Playing with my princesses is lots of fun for me.
I just love cheese on toast to eat,
And sometimes a cookie for a treat.
Green is a colour I like a lot,
My set of Peppa Pig toys is the best present I ever got.
My favourite person is Mummy, who is a gem,
So this, my first poem, is just for them!

Alyssa Anne Standhaven (3)
Barugh Green Preschool, Barnsley

# My First Poem

My name is Merryn and I go to preschool,
My best friend is Sasha, who is really cool.
I watch Frozen on TV,
Playing on the trampoline is lots of fun for me.
I just love Coco Pops to eat,
And sometimes a Chomp for a treat.
Green is a colour I like a lot,
My Frozen jigsaw is the best present I ever got.
My favourite person is Adam, my brother, who is a gem,
So this, my first poem, is just for them!

Merryn Harper (3)
Barugh Green Preschool, Barnsley

# My First Poem

My name is Ruby and I go to preschool,
My best friend is Ellie, who is really cool.
I watch Tangled on TV,
Playing babies is lots of fun for me.
I just love pasta to eat,
And sometimes Smarties for a treat.
Red is a colour I like a lot,
My kitchen is the best present I ever got.
My favourite person is Mummy, who is a gem,
So this, my first poem, is just for them!

Ruby Lister (4)
Barugh Green Preschool, Barnsley

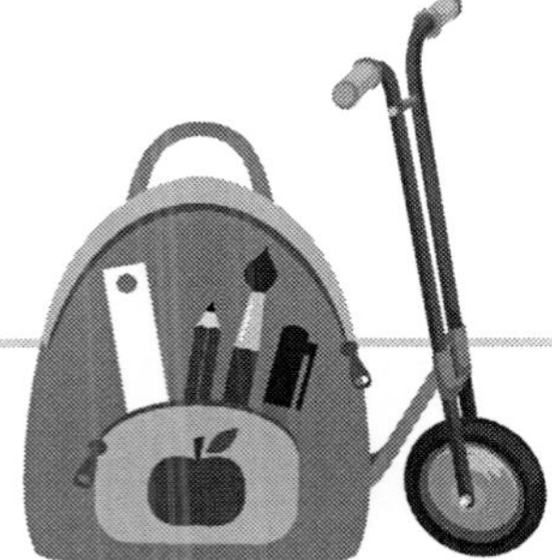

# My First Poem

My name is Sarah and I go to preschool,
My best friend is Sarah, who is really cool.
I watch CBeebies on TV,
Playing with my Harry doll is lots of fun for me.
I just love fish fingers to eat,
And sometimes I get chocolate for a treat.
Black is a colour I like a lot,
My One Direction cover is the best present I ever got.
My favourite person is my nanny, who is a gem,
So this, my first poem, is just for them!

Sarah McKevitt (4)
Child's Play Preschool, Banbridge

# My First Poem

My name is Conor and I go to preschool,
My best friend is Harry, who is really cool.
I watch lots on TV,
Playing with Lego is lots of fun for me.
I just love chips to eat,
And sometimes I get chocolate for a treat.
Blue is a colour I like a lot,
My Lego is the best present I ever got.
My favourite person is my mummy, who is a gem,
So this, my first poem, is just for them!

Conor Rogan (3)
Child's Play Preschool, Banbridge

# My First Poem

My name is Carla and I go to preschool,
My best friend is Rossa, who is really cool.
I watch The Mask on TV,
Playing with Mummy and Daddy is lots of fun for me.
I just love pizza to eat,
And sometimes I eat lollipops and marshmallows for a treat.
Pink is a colour I like a lot,
My new doll is the best present I ever got.
My favourite person is my mummy, who is a gem,
So this, my first poem, is just for them!

Carla Frampton (4)
Child's Play Preschool, Banbridge

# My First Poem

My name is Lily and I go to preschool,
My best friend is Sophie, who is really cool.
I watch My Little Pony on TV,
Playing with Snow Glow Elsa is lots of fun for me.
I just love chips and gravy to eat,
And sometimes mint Aero for a treat.
Rainbow is a colour I like a lot,
My sparkle cat is the best present I ever got.
My favourite person is Ethel, who is a gem,
So this, my first poem, is just for them!

Lily Nelson (4)
Dervock Community Playgroup, Ballymoney

# My First Poem

My name is Tanisha and I go to preschool,
My best friend is Sophie, who is really cool.
I watch Peppa Pig on TV,
Playing with jigsaws is lots of fun for me.
I just love dinner to eat,
And sometimes sweets for a treat.
Pink is a colour I like a lot,
My new Peppa Pig book is the best present I ever got.
My favourite person is Mummy, who is a gem,
So this, my first poem, is just for them!

Tanisha Hutchinson (4)
Dervock Community Playgroup, Ballymoney

# My First Poem

My name is Holly and I go to preschool,
My best friend is Riley, who is really cool.
I watch Spider-Man on TV,
Playing with my dog is lots of fun for me.
I just love chips and peas to eat,
And sometimes chewing gum for a treat.
Blue is a colour I like a lot,
My Spider-Man toy is the best present I ever got.
My favourite person is Amy, who is a gem,
So this, my first poem, is just for them!

Holly Walsh (4)
Dervock Community Playgroup, Ballymoney

# My First Poem

My name is Poppy and I go to preschool,
My best friend is Riley, who is really cool.
I watch Tiny Pop on TV,
Playing on my scooter is lots of fun for me.
I just love sausages and chips to eat,
And sometimes chocolate bars for a treat.
Blue is a colour I like a lot,
My scooter is the best present I ever got.
My favourite person is Sophie, who is a gem,
So this, my first poem, is just for them!

Poppy Coulter (4)
Dervock Community Playgroup, Ballymoney

# My First Poem

My name is Ryan and I go to preschool,
My best friend is Sophie, who is really cool.
I watch Numberjacks on TV,
Playing with gummy bears is lots of fun for me.
I just love onion rings to eat,
And sometimes fudge bars for a treat.
White is a colour I like a lot,
My Luigi teddy is the best present I ever got.
My favourite person is Glenn, who is a gem,
So this, my first poem, is just for them!

Ryan Nelson (4)
Dervock Community Playgroup, Ballymoney

# My First Poem

My name is Sophie and I go to preschool,
My best friend is Lily, who is really cool.
I watch Mr Bean on TV,
Playing on my trampoline is lots of fun for me.
I just love custard to eat,
And sometimes Freddo bars for a treat.
Blue is a colour I like a lot,
My Minion teddy is the best present I ever got.
My favourite person is Ethel, who is a gem,
So this, my first poem, is just for them!

Sophie Walker (4)
Dervock Community Playgroup, Ballymoney

# My First Poem

My name is Grace and I go to preschool,
My best friend is Savannah, who is really cool.
I watch Dora on TV,
Playing with my Peppa Pig is lots of fun for me.
I just love burgers and chicken to eat,
And sometimes chocolate eggs for a treat.
Pink is a colour I like a lot,
My blue pony is the best present I ever got.
My favourite person is Jack, who is a gem,
So this, my first poem, is just for them!

Grace McMullan (4)
Dervock Community Playgroup, Ballymoney

# My First Poem

My name is Savannah and I go to preschool,
My best friend is Grace, who is really cool.
I watch Scooby-Doo on TV,
Playing on my bike is lots of fun for me.
I just love chicken nuggets and gravy to eat,
And sometimes ice cream for a treat.
Pink is a colour I like a lot,
My stuffed dog is the best present I ever got.
My favourite person is Mammy, who is a gem,
So this, my first poem, is just for them!

Savannah White (4)
Dervock Community Playgroup, Ballymoney

# My First Poem

My name is Haydn and I go to preschool,
My best friend is Grace, who is really cool.
I watch Tom and Jerry on TV,
Playing The Lego Movie game is lots of fun for me.
I just love pasta to eat,
And sometimes sweeties for a treat.
Green is a colour I like a lot,
My Shopkins is the best present I ever got.
My favourite person is Daddy, who is a gem,
So this, my first poem, is just for them!

Haydn Harkness (4)
Dervock Community Playgroup, Ballymoney

# My First Poem

My name is Alfie and I go to preschool,
My best friend is Nanny, who is really cool.
I watch Peppa Pig and Ben & Holly on TV,
Playing with Lego is lots of fun for me.
I just love chips to eat,
And sometimes a Chinese for a treat.
Red is a colour I like a lot,
My washing machine is the best present I ever got.
My favourite person is Jak, my little brother, who
is a gem,
So this, my first poem, is just for them!

Alfie McMaster (4)
Dervock Community Playgroup, Ballymoney

# My First Poem

My name is Riley and I go to preschool,
My best friend is Holly, who is really cool.
I watch Batman on TV,
Playing The Lego Movie game is lots of fun for me.
I just love chips to eat,
And sometimes pizza for a treat.
Blue is a colour I like a lot,
My Spider-Man motorbike is the best present I ever got.
My favourite person is Jake, my brother, who is a gem,
So this, my first poem, is just for them!

Riley Thompson (4)
Dervock Community Playgroup, Ballymoney

# My First Poem

My name is Brennin and I go to preschool,
My best friend is my brother, Ryan, who is really cool.
I watch Sofia and Dora on TV,
Playing silly dances in the rain is lots of fun for me.
I just love cheese and garlic bread to eat,
And sometimes jelly babies for a treat.
Yellow is a colour I like a lot,
My Peppa Pig plane is the best present I ever got.
My favourite person is my mum, who is a gem,
So this, my first poem, is just for them!

Brennin O'Hara (3)
Happy Tots Playgroup, Lisburn

# My First Poem

My name is Ruairi and I go to preschool,
My best friend is Séan, who is really cool.
I watch Aquabats Supershow on TV,
Playing in the water is lots of fun for me.
I just love fajitas to eat,
And sometimes fudge for a treat.
Blue is a colour I like a lot,
My Scooby-Doo board game is the best present I ever got.
My favourite person is my friend, Leon, who is a gem,
So this, my first poem, is just for them!

Ruairi Docherty (4)
Hillcrest Day Nursery, Belfast

# My First Poem

My name is Jackson and I go to preschool,
My best friend is James, who is really cool.
I watch SpongeBob on TV,
Playing Spider-Man and the Hulk is lots of fun for me.
I just love spuds to eat,
And sometimes chocolate for a treat.
Brown is a colour I like a lot,
My Mousetrap game is the best present I ever got.
My favourite person is Jude, who is a gem,
So this, my first poem, is just for them!

Jackson Lonergan (4)
Hillcrest Day Nursery, Belfast

# My First Poem

My name is Joseph and I go to preschool,
My best friend is Leo, who is really cool.
I watch Spider-Man on TV,
Playing with Lego is lots of fun for me.
I just love fish pie to eat,
And sometimes ice lollies for a treat.
Red is a colour I like a lot,
My Doctor Octopus is the best present I ever got.
My favourite person is Mummy, who is a gem,
So this, my first poem, is just for them!

Joseph McGivern (4)
Hillcrest Day Nursery, Belfast

# My First Poem

My name is Olly and I go to preschool,
My best friend is Jacob, who is really cool.
I watch Spider-Man on TV,
Playing Batman is lots of fun for me.
I just love fish fingers to eat,
And sometimes everything, I love sweeties for a treat.
Red is a colour I like a lot,
My football table is the best present I ever got.
My favourite person is Charlie, who is a gem,
So this, my first poem, is just for them!

Olly Murphy
Hillcrest Day Nursery, Belfast

# My First Poem

My name is Jessica and I go to preschool,
My best friend is Avelyn, who is really cool.
I watch Peppa Pig on TV,
Playing with my sister is lots of fun for me.
I just love pasta to eat,
And sometimes sweets and chocolate for a treat.
Pink is a colour I like a lot,
My Tiny Tears dolly is the best present I ever got.
My favourite person is my daddy, who is a gem,
So this, my first poem, is just for them!

Jessica Batiste (3)
Hillside Preschool, Guernsey

# My First Poem

My name is Aisling and I go to preschool,
My best friend is Amie, who is really cool.
I watch Balamory on TV,
Playing snakes and ladders is lots of fun for me.
I just love a red apple to eat,
And sometimes biscuits for a treat.
Pink is a colour I like a lot,
My Baby Annabell is the best present I ever got.
My favourite person is Daddy, who is a gem,
So this, my first poem, is just for them!

Aisling Ryan (3)
Hillside Preschool, Guernsey

# My First Poem

My name is Cody and I go to preschool,
My best friend is Danny, who is really cool.
I watch PAW Patrol on TV,
Playing with Playmobil is lots of fun for me.
I just love potatoes to eat,
And sometimes chocolate buttons for a treat.
Blue is a colour I like a lot,
My off-road Lightning McQueen is the best
present I ever got.
My favourite person is Mummy, who is a gem,
So this, my first poem, is just for them!

Cody Jensen Lowe (3)
Hillside Preschool, Guernsey

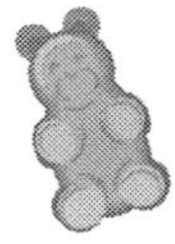

# My First Poem

My name is Lily and I go to preschool,
My best friend is Belle, who is really cool.
I watch Peppa Pig on TV,
Playing with my friends is lots of fun for me.
I just love breadsticks and fruit to eat,
And sometimes chocolate lollies for a treat.
Red is a colour I like a lot,
My bike is the best present I ever got.
My favourite person is Mummy, who is a gem,
So this, my first poem, is just for them!

Lily Knott (2)
Hillside Preschool, Guernsey

# My First Poem

My name is Avelyn and I go to preschool,
My best friend is Ruby, who is really cool.
I watch Frozen on TV,
Playing with the Barbies and in the home corner is lots of fun for me.
I just love fish and chips to eat,
And sometimes chocolate for a treat.
Pink is a colour I like a lot,
My Frozen fur coat is the best present I ever got.
My favourite person is Daddy, who is a gem,
So this, my first poem, is just for them!

Avelyn Hilley (4)
Hillside Preschool, Guernsey

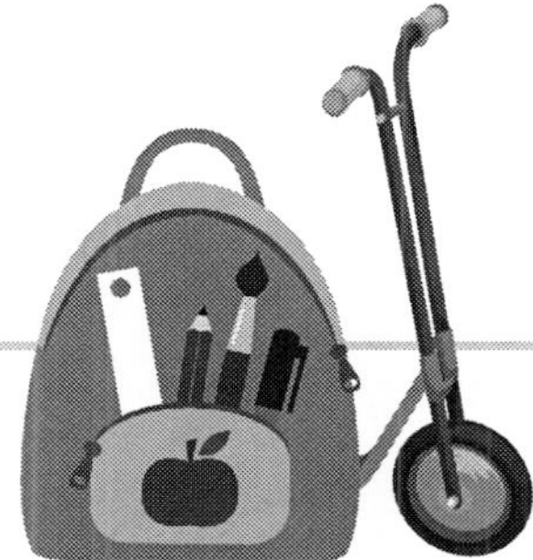

# My First Poem

My name is Robert and I go to preschool,
My best friend is Alexis, who is really cool.
I watch the pups from PAW Patrol on TV,
Playing with my trains and cars is lots of fun for me.
I just love fish fingers, chips and fruit to eat,
And sometimes ice cream or a lolly for a treat.
Red and white makes pink, it is a colour I like a lot,
My Haunted House pop-up book is the best present I ever got.
My favourite person is my daddy, who is a gem,
So this, my first poem, is just for them!

Robert Kelly (3)
Hillside Preschool, Guernsey

# My First Poem

My name is Jasmine and I go to preschool,
My best friend is Eden, who is really cool.
I watch Barbie on TV,
Playing with Barbies is lots of fun for me.
I just love chicken to eat,
And sometimes chocolate for a treat.
Pink is a colour I like a lot,
My Barbie bike is the best present I ever got.
My favourite person is Mummy, who is a gem,
So this, my first poem, is just for them!

Jasmine Daisy Ferbrache-De Cartaret (4)
Hillside Preschool, Guernsey

# My First Poem

My name is Emilie and I go to preschool,
My best friend is my mummy, who is really cool.
I watch Doc McStuffins on TV,
Playing with my dolls is lots of fun for me.
I just love spaghetti Bolognese to eat,
And sometimes chocolate cake for a treat.
Pink is a colour I like a lot,
My Lambie doll is the best present I ever got.
My favourite person is Mummy, who is a gem,
So this, my first poem, is just for them!

Emilie Miller (3)
Hillside Preschool, Guernsey

# My First Poem

My name is Amie and I go to preschool,
My best friend is Avelyn, who is really cool.
I watch Doc McStuffins on TV,
Playing with my Sylvanians is lots of fun for me.
I just love pizza to eat,
And sometimes Party Rings for a treat.
Purple is a colour I like a lot,
My Hallie doll is the best present I ever got.
My favourite person is Daddy, who is a gem,
So this, my first poem, is just for them!

Amie Miller (5)
Hillside Preschool, Guernsey

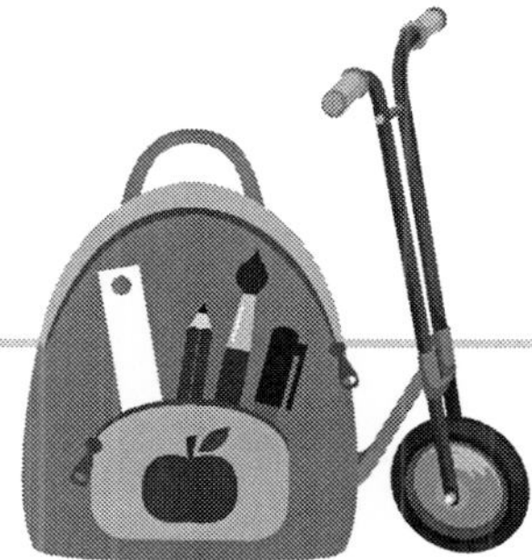

# My First Poem

My name is Charlotte and I go to preschool,
My best friend is Max, who is really cool.
I watch CBeebies on TV,
Playing on my trampoline is lots of fun for me.
I just love cucumber, pasta and chocolate to eat,
And sometimes meringues and cream for a treat.
Pink is a colour I like a lot,
My Frozen Elsa dress is the best present I ever got.
My favourite person is my Daddy, who is a gem,
So this, my first poem, is just for them!

Charlotte Lydia Gallienne (4)
Hillside Preschool, Guernsey

# My First Poem

My name is Joshua and I go to preschool,
My best friend is Jack, who is really cool.
I watch Fireman Sam on TV,
Playing hide-and-seek is lots of fun for me.
I just love sausage and chips with sauce to eat,
And sometimes chocolate for a treat.
Orange is a colour I like a lot,
My yellow car is the best present I ever got.
My favourite person is Daddy, who is a gem,
So this, my first poem, is just for them!

Joshua Stuart (2)
Hillside Preschool, Guernsey

# My First Poem

My name is Aleisha-Mae and I go to preschool,
My best friend is Marley, who is really cool.
I watch Fireman Sam on TV,
Playing with dollies and babies is lots of fun for me.
I just love cheese to eat,
And sometimes chocolate biscuits for a treat.
Blue is a colour I like a lot,
My giant Peppa Pig is the best present I ever got.
My favourite person is my big sister, Charlie, who is a gem,
So this, my first poem, is just for them!

Aleisha-Mae Guilbert (2)
Hillside Preschool, Guernsey

# My First Poem

My name is Aaron and I go to preschool,
My best friend is Ruby, who is really cool.
I watch Fireman Sam on TV,
Playing with trucks and tractors is lots of fun for me.
I just love sausages to eat,
And sometimes chocolate for a treat.
Yellow is a colour I like a lot,
My crane is the best present I ever got.
My favourite person is Mummy, who is a gem,
So this, my first poem, is just for them!

Aaron Loveridge (3)
Hillside Preschool, Guernsey

# My First Poem

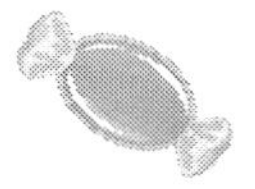

My name is Maximus and I go to preschool,
My best friend is Brandon, who is really cool.
I watch Sheriff Callie on TV,
Playing with puzzles is lots of fun for me.
I just love waffles to eat,
And sometimes chocolate for a treat.
Blue is a colour I like a lot,
My Play-Doh is the best present I ever got.
My favourite person is Jesse, who is a gem,
So this, my first poem, is just for them!

Maximus Kendall (2)
Hillside Preschool, Guernsey

# My First Poem

My name is Danny and I go to preschool,
My best friend is Cody, who is really cool.
I watch Fireman Sam on TV,
Playing and running around is lots of fun for me.
I just love toast to eat,
And sometimes strawberry laces for a treat.
Orange is a colour I like a lot,
My balloon pump is the best present I ever got.
My favourite person is Mummy, who is a gem,
So this, my first poem, is just for them!

Danny King (3)
Hillside Preschool, Guernsey

# My First Poem

My name is Ben and I go to preschool,
My best friend is everyone at Hillside, who is really cool.
I watch PAW Patrol on TV,
Playing my Pirate Pursuit game is lots of fun for me.
I just love sandwiches to eat,
And sometimes chocolate eggs for a treat.
Red is a colour I like a lot,
My Octonauts Gup-B is the best present I ever got.
My favourite person is Mummy, who is a gem,
So this, my first poem, is just for them!

Benjamin Holland (4)
Hillside Preschool, Guernsey

# My First Poem

My name is Eden and I go to preschool,
My best friend is Jasmine, who is really cool.
I watch Sleeping Beauty on TV,
Playing with Playmobil fairies is lots of fun for me.
I just love pasta to eat,
And sometimes ice cream for a treat.
Pink is a colour I like a lot,
My pretty dress is the best present I ever got.
My favourite person is Mummy, who is a gem,
So this, my first poem, is just for them!

Eden Phoebe Smith (4)
Hillside Preschool, Guernsey

# My First Poem

My name is Brandon and I go to preschool,
My best friend is Robbie, who is really cool.
I watch PAW Patrol on TV,
Playing with cars is lots of fun for me.
I just love sausage and chips to eat,
And sometimes jaffa cakes for a treat.
Green is a colour I like a lot,
My swing is the best present I ever got.
My favourite person is Mummy, who is a gem,
So this, my first poem, is just for them!

Brandon Corbet (2)
Hillside Preschool, Guernsey

# My First Poem

My name is Zachary and I go to preschool,
My best friend is Cody, who is really cool.
I watch Curious George on TV,
Playing with cars is lots of fun for me.
I just love spaghetti Bolognese to eat,
And sometimes cake for a treat.
Blue is a colour I like a lot,
My Lego fire station is the best present I ever got.
My favourite person is Joshua, who is a gem,
So this, my first poem, is just for them!

Zachary Davison (3)
Hillside Preschool, Guernsey

# My First Poem

My name is Ebenezer and I go to preschool,
My best friend is Eden, who is really cool.
I watch PAW Patrol on TV,
Playing with Lego is lots of fun for me.
I just love cottage pie to eat,
And sometimes chocolate for a treat.
Red is a colour I like a lot,
My guitar from Aunty Kor is the best present I ever got.
My favourite people are Mummy and Daddy, who are gems,
So this, my first poem, is just for them!

Ebenezer Le Page (4)
Hillside Preschool, Guernsey

# My First Poem

My name is Jake and I go to preschool,
My best friend is Brandon, who is really cool.
I watch cartoons on TV,
Playing with cars is lots of fun for me.
I just love jam sandwiches to eat,
And sometimes chocolate biscuits for a treat.
Orange is a colour I like a lot,
My blue scooter is the best present I ever got.
My favourite person is Brandon, who is a gem,
So this, my first poem, is just for them!

Jake Goupillot (2)
Hillside Preschool, Guernsey

# My First Poem

My name is Daisy and I go to preschool,
My best friend is Avelyn, who is really cool.
I watch Rapunzel on TV,
Playing with Hama beads is lots of fun for me.
I just love pasta to eat,
And sometimes chocolate ice cream for a treat.
Red is a colour I like a lot,
My cuddly Olaf is the best present I ever got.
My favourite person is Daddy, who is a gem,
So this, my first poem, is just for them!

Daisy Aylmer
Hillside Preschool, Guernsey

# My First Poem

My name is Ryan and I go to preschool,
My best friend is Freddie, who is really cool.
I watch Spider-Man and Batman on TV,
Playing Super Mario and Minecraft is lots of fun for me.
I just love cheesy pizza to eat,
And sometimes a chocolate Wispa bar for a treat.
Dinosaur green is a colour I like a lot,
My little pet bird is the best present I ever got.
My favourite person is my brother, Owen, who is a gem,
So this, my first poem, is just for them!

Ryan Colling (4)
Hillside Preschool, Guernsey

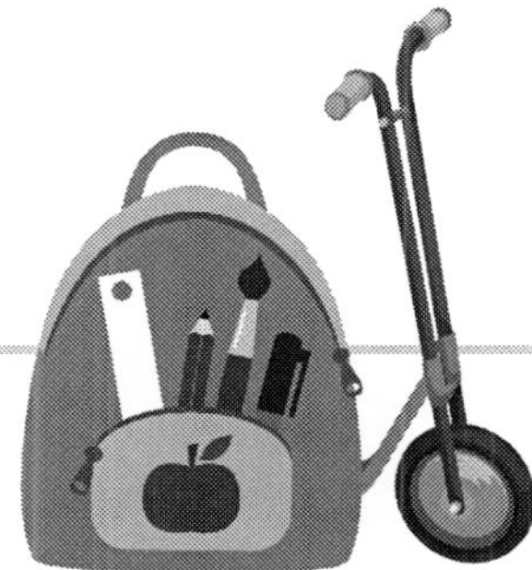

# My First Poem

My name is Robbie and I go to preschool,
My best friend is Avelyn, who is really cool.
I watch Andy's Dinosaur Adventures on TV,
Playing and racing cars is lots of fun for me.
I just love chicken nuggets to eat,
And sometimes lollipops and golden barrels for a treat.
Blue is a colour I like a lot,
My triceratops is the best present I ever got.
My favourite person is my sister, Georgia, who is a gem,
So this, my first poem, is just for them!

Robbie Harvey (2)
Hillside Preschool, Guernsey

# My First Poem

My name is Ella and I go to preschool,
My best friend is Belle, who is really cool.
I watch Peppa Pig on TV,
Playing with dollies is lots of fun for me.
I just love rice to eat,
And sometimes chocolate for a treat.
Pink is a colour I like a lot,
My doll's pram is the best present I ever got.
My favourite person is Mummy, who is a gem,
So this, my first poem, is just for them!

Ella Gallienne (2)
Hillside Preschool, Guernsey

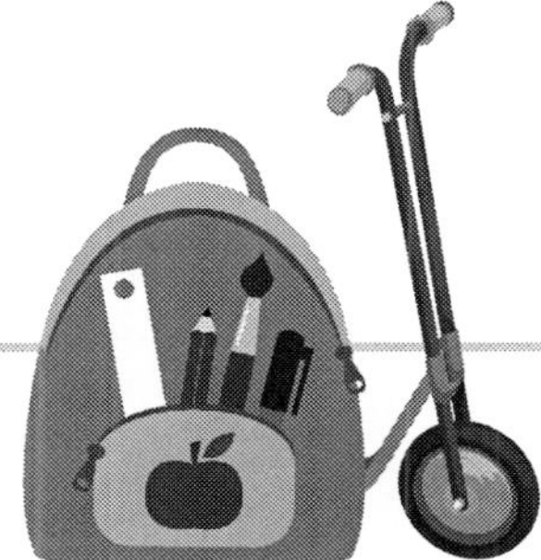

# My First Poem

My name is Daisy and I go to preschool,
My best friend is Aaliyah, who is really cool.
I watch Sofia the First on TV,
Playing with Play-Doh and dressing up is lots of fun for me.
I just love gnocchi with pesto sauce to eat,
And sometimes sausages and mash for a treat.
Indigo is a colour I like a lot,
My Mr Men sparkly book set is the best present I ever got.
My favourite person is my baby sister, Alice, who is a gem,
So this, my first poem, is just for them!

Daisy Clarkson (2)
Hillside Preschool, Guernsey

# My First Poem

My name is Micah and I go to preschool,
My best friend is Eden, who is really cool.
I watch dinosaurs on TV,
Playing with dinosaurs is lots of fun for me.
I just love chicken to eat,
And sometimes biscuits for a treat.
Blue is a colour I like a lot,
My sharp tooth dinosaur is the best present I ever got.
My favourite person is Mummy, who is a gem,
So this, my first poem, is just for them!

Micah Gannon (2)
Hillside Preschool, Guernsey

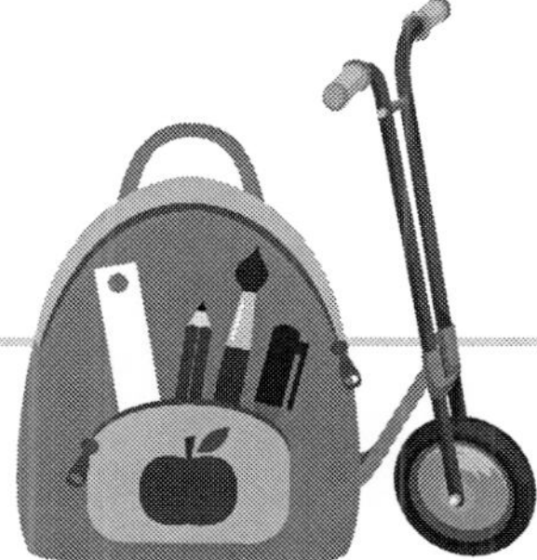

# My First Poem

My name is Eden and I go to preschool,
My best friend is Micah, who is really cool.
I watch Frozen on TV,
Playing with my scooter and dolls is lots of fun for me.
I just love Bolognese to eat,
And sometimes chips for a treat.
Yellow is a colour I like a lot,
My Baby Pippin is the best present I ever got.
My favourite person is Mummy, who is a gem,
So this, my first poem, is just for them!

Eden Gannon (4)
Hillside Preschool, Guernsey

# My First Poem

My name is Daniel and I go to preschool,
My best friend is Zach, who is really cool.
I watch the Ninja Turtles on TV,
Playing doctors with my sister is lots of fun for me.
I just love pizza and hot dogs to eat,
And sometimes Love Heart sweeties for a treat.
Bright pink is a colour I like a lot,
My Spider-Man shooting gun is the best present I ever got.
My favourite person is Mummy, who is a gem,
So this, my first poem, is just for them!

Daniel Bell (3)
Hillside Preschool, Guernsey

# My First Poem

My name is Cara and I go to preschool,
My best friend is Rosie, who is really cool.
I watch Dora on TV,
Playing my piano is lots of fun for me.
I just love chicken nuggets and chips to eat,
And sometimes red sweeties for a treat.
Blue is a colour I like a lot,
My doll is the best present I ever got.
My favourite person is my brother, who is a gem,
So this, my first poem, is just for them!

Cara Haughey (3)
Little Friends Playgroup, Omagh

# My First Poem

My name is Daithi and I go to preschool,
My best friend is Seth, who is really cool.
I watch Fireman Sam on TV,
Playing with my fire engine is lots of fun for me.
I just love sausages to eat,
And sometimes carrot sweeties for a treat.
Red is a colour I like a lot,
My fire engine is the best present I ever got.
My favourite person is Daddy, who is a gem,
So this, my first poem, is just for them!

Daithi Ciaran Bernard Gallagher (3)
Little Friends Playgroup, Omagh

# My First Poem

My name is Eliana and I go to preschool,
My best friend is Nuala, who is really cool.
I watch Mia and Bo On the Go on TV,
Playing Number Fly is lots of fun for me.
I just love broccoli to eat,
And sometimes chocolate for a treat.
Pink is a colour I like a lot,
My tree house is the best present I ever got.
My favourite person is Mummy, who is a gem,
So this, my first poem, is just for them!

Eliana McKenna (3)
Little Friends Playgroup, Omagh

# My First Poem

My name is Rosie and I go to preschool,
My best friend is Eabha-Rose, who is really cool.
I watch Peppa Pig on TV,
Playing with teddies is lots of fun for me.
I just love spuds to eat,
And sometimes jelly babies for a treat.
Pink is a colour I like a lot,
My doll is the best present I ever got.
My favourite person is Mummy, who is a gem,
So this, my first poem, is just for them!

Rosie May Clarke (3)
Little Friends Playgroup, Omagh

# My First Poem

My name is Charlie and I go to preschool,
My best friend is Malachy, who is really cool.
I watch Thomas on TV,
Playing with trains is lots of fun for me.
I just love grapes to eat,
And sometimes sweeties for a treat.
Red is a colour I like a lot,
My play dough is the best present I ever got.
My favourite person is my mummy, who is a gem,
So this, my first poem, is just for them!

Charlie McNabb (3)
Little Friends Playgroup, Omagh

# My First Poem

My name is Malachy and I go to preschool,
My best friend is Charlie, who is really cool.
I watch Go Go Thomas on TV,
Playing with my Polar Express train is lots of fun for me.
I just love pancakes to eat,
And sometimes a Milky Way for a treat.
Yellow is a colour I like a lot,
My Postman Pat helicopter is the best present I ever got.
My favourite person is Finn, who is a gem,
So this, my first poem, is just for them!

Malachy McGillin (4)
Little Friends Playgroup, Omagh

# My First Poem

My name is Christy and I go to preschool,
My best friend is Seth, who is really cool.
I watch Mr Bean on TV,
Playing hide-and-seek is lots of fun for me.
I just love bacon to eat,
And sometimes lollipops for a treat.
Green is a colour I like a lot,
My car with Woody and Buzz is the best present I ever got.
My favourite person is my mummy, who is a gem,
So this, my first poem, is just for them!

Christy Johnston (3)
Little Friends Playgroup, Omagh

# My First Poem

My name is Jamie and I go to preschool,
My best friend is Riley, who is really cool.
I watch Thomas on TV,
Playing with cars is lots of fun for me.
I just love sandwiches to eat,
And sometimes sweets for a treat.
Green is a colour I like a lot,
My train set is the best present I ever got.
My favourite person is Mummy, who is a gem,
So this, my first poem, is just for them!

Jamie Hetherington (3)
Little Friends Playgroup, Omagh

# My First Poem

My name is Eabha-Rose and I go to preschool,
My best friend is Rosie, who is really cool.
I watch Mickey Mouse on TV,
Playing with dollies is lots of fun for me.
I just love sausage and chips to eat,
And sometimes sweeties for a treat.
Pink is a colour I like a lot,
My dress is the best present I ever got.
My favourite person is Mummy, who is a gem,
So this, my first poem, is just for them!

Eabha-Rose McDaid Donnelly (4)
Little Friends Playgroup, Omagh

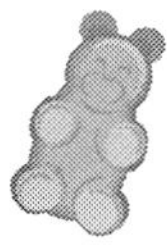

# My First Poem

My name is Aoibhin and I go to preschool,
My best friend is my mummy, who is really cool.
I watch Sheriff Callie on TV,
Playing with dolls is lots of fun for me.
I just love sandwiches to eat,
And sometimes chocolate bars for a treat.
Red is a colour I like a lot,
My dolly is the best present I ever got.
My favourite person is Aine, who is a gem,
So this, my first poem, is just for them!

Aoibhin McNabb Woods (3)
Little Friends Playgroup, Omagh

# My First Poem

My name is Riley and I go to preschool,
My best friend is Conall, who is really cool.
I watch Disney on TV,
Playing with my Blade Ranger helicopter is lots of fun for me.
I just love chicken nuggets and chips to eat,
And sometimes chocolate eggs for a treat.
Green is a colour I like a lot,
My green helicopter is the best present I ever got.
My favourite person is Mummy, who is a gem,
So this, my first poem, is just for them!

Riley McLaughlin (3)
Little Friends Playgroup, Omagh

# My First Poem

My name is Conor and I go to preschool,
My best friend is Nuala, who is really cool.
I watch football on TV,
Playing football is lots of fun for me.
I just love sausages to eat,
And sometimes crisps for a treat.
Blue is a colour I like a lot,
My green tractor is the best present I ever got.
My favourite person is Daddy, who is a gem,
So this, my first poem, is just for them!

Conor Murray (3)
Little Friends Playgroup, Omagh

# My First Poem

My name is Nuala and I go to preschool,
My best friend is Eabha-Rose, who is really cool.
I watch Peppa Pig on TV,
Playing Buckaroo is lots of fun for me.
I just love sausages to eat,
And sometimes a chocolate bar with cream for a treat.
Pink is a colour I like a lot,
My Jessie is the best present I ever got.
My favourite person is my mummy, who is a gem,
So this, my first poem, is just for them!

Nuala O'Neill (3)
Little Friends Playgroup, Omagh

# My First Poem

My name is Conall and I go to preschool,
My best friend is Riley, who is really cool.
I watch Horrid Henry on TV,
Playing with cars is lots of fun for me.
I just love milky ice cream to eat,
And sometimes chocolate bars for a treat.
Blue is a colour I like a lot,
My aeroplane is the best present I ever got.
My favourite person is Dara, my baby brother,
who is a gem,
So this, my first poem, is just for them!

Conall McCaffrey (3)
Little Friends Playgroup, Omagh

# My First Poem

My name is Ronan and I go to preschool,
My best friend is Riley, who is really cool.
I watch Thomas on TV,
Playing with my Thomas choo choo trains is
lots of fun for me.
I just love Weetabix to eat,
And sometimes Maltesers for a treat.
Green is a colour I like a lot,
My Hot Wheels track is the best present I ever got.
My favourite person is Mummy, who is a gem,
So this, my first poem, is just for them!

Ronan Nugent (4)
Little Friends Playgroup, Omagh

# My First Poem

My name is Fintan and I go to preschool,
My best friend is Malachy, who is really cool.
I watch a Santa DVD on TV,
Playing with my dragon is lots of fun for me.
I just love lasagne to eat,
And sometimes chocolate for a treat.
Green is a colour I like a lot,
My dragon is the best present I ever got.
My favourite person is Mummy, who is a gem,
So this, my first poem, is just for them!

Fintan James Kearney (3)
Little Friends Playgroup, Omagh

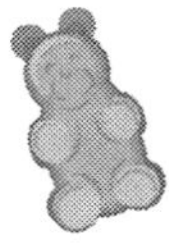

# My First Poem

My name is Mya-Isabella and I go to preschool,
My best friend is Victoria, who is really cool.
I watch Bing on TV,
Playing with dolls and dressing up is lots of fun for me.
I just love fruit, sandwiches and Mummy's home-made curry to eat,
And sometimes sweets and ice cream for a treat.
Red is a colour I like a lot,
My Frozen Elsa doll is the best present I ever got.
My favourite person is Uncle Andrew, who is a gem,
So this, my first poem, is just for them!

Mya-Isabella Close (4)
Little Friends Preschool, Banbridge

# My First Poem

My name is Michael and I go to preschool,
My best friend is Nathan, who is really cool.
I watch SpongeBob SquarePants on TV,
Playing with my Batman toys is lots of fun for me.
I just love burgers and red sauce to eat,
And sometimes sweeties for a treat.
Red is a colour I like a lot,
My PlayStation game is the best present I ever got.
My favourite person is Mummy, who is a gem,
So this, my first poem, is just for them!

Michael Toal (4)
Little Friends Preschool, Banbridge

# My First Poem

My name is Orlágh and I go to preschool,
My best friend is Elena, who is really cool.
I watch funny things on TV,
Playing mummies is lots of fun for me.
I just love potatoes and mince to eat,
And sometimes sweets for a treat.
Green is a colour I like a lot,
My bicycle is the best present I ever got.
My favourite person is my mummy, who is a gem,
So this, my first poem, is just for them!

Orlágh Doherty (4)
Little Friends Preschool, Banbridge

# My First Poem

My name is Lily-Ella and I go to preschool,
My best friend is Erin, who is really cool.
I watch Curious George on TV,
Playing in the sand is lots of fun for me.
I just love pancakes to eat,
And sometimes lollies for a treat.
Purple is a colour I like a lot,
My Elsa doll is the best present I ever got.
My favourite person is Mummy, who is a gem,
So this, my first poem, is just for them!

Lily-Ella Dale (4)
Little Friends Preschool, Banbridge

# My First Poem

My name is Corey and I go to preschool,
My best friend is Emily, who is really cool.
I watch Peppa Pig on TV,
Playing outside with friends is lots of fun for me.
I just love chicken and chips to eat,
And sometimes a Kinder egg for a treat.
Blue is a colour I like a lot,
My bike is the best present I ever got.
My favourite person is Mummy, who is a gem,
So this, my first poem, is just for them!

Corey Lynch (4)
Little Friends Preschool, Banbridge

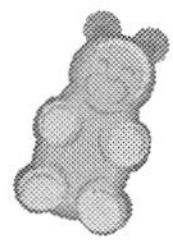

# My First Poem

My name is Jude and I go to preschool,
My best friend is Luke, who is really cool.
I watch Peppa Pig and PAW Patrol on TV,
Playing with my race cars and chasing is lots of fun for me.
I just love cucumber, carrots and fruit to eat,
And sometimes sweets and ice cream for a treat.
Blue is a colour I like a lot,
My trampoline is the best present I ever got.
My favourite person is my mummy, who is a gem,
So this, my first poem, is just for them!

Jude Madeley (4)
Little Friends Preschool, Banbridge

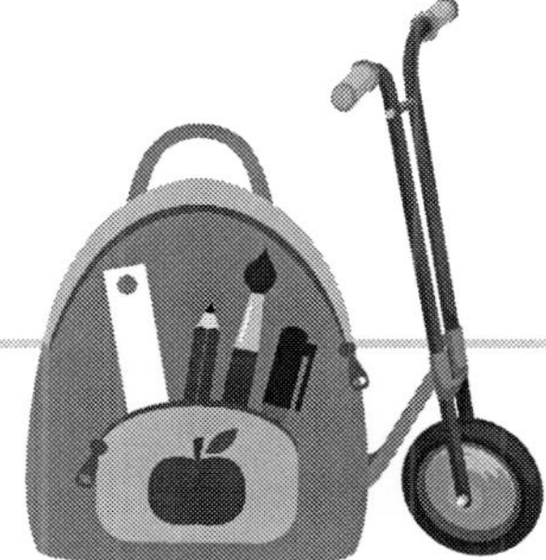

# My First Poem

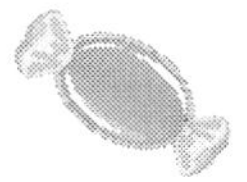

My name is Nathan and I go to preschool,
My best friend is my big brother, Evan, who is really cool.
I watch Postman Pat and Fireman Sam on TV,
Playing with my cars and trucks is lots of fun for me.
I just love pasta shapes and sauce to eat,
And sometimes chocolate buns and chips for a treat.
Green is a colour I like a lot,
My fire station is the best present I ever got.
My favourite person is my mummy, who is a gem,
So this, my first poem, is just for them!

Nathan Moore (4)
Little Friends Preschool, Banbridge

# My First Poem

My name is Dylan and I go to preschool,
My best friend is Mark, who is really cool.
I watch Thomas and Friends on TV,
Playing with Thomas and Friends trains is lots of fun for me.
I just love drumsticks to eat,
And sometimes a chocolate egg for a treat.
Blue is a colour I like a lot,
My Buzz Lightyear is the best present I ever got.
My favourite person is Amber, who is a gem,
So this, my first poem, is just for them!

Dylan Frederick Robert Charters (4)
Little Friends Preschool, Banbridge

# My First Poem

My name is Daniel and I go to preschool,
My best friend is Aimee, who is really cool.
I watch Toy Story and Inspector Gadget on TV,
Playing in the sand and with Play-Doh is lots of fun for me.
I just love Nannie's potatoes to eat,
And sometimes biscuits for a treat.
Green is a colour I like a lot,
My Buzz Lightyear is the best present I ever got.
My favourite person is Levi, my baby cousin, who is a gem,
So this, my first poem, is just for them!

Daniel Edmond David Ferguson (4)
Little Friends Preschool, Banbridge

# My First Poem

My name is Joshua and I go to preschool,
My best friend is George, who is really cool.
I watch scary monsters on TV,
Playing with Spider-Man is lots of fun for me.
I just love chicken and chips to eat,
And sometimes chocolate for a treat.
Blue is a colour I like a lot,
My bike is the best present I ever got.
My favourite person is Harvey, who is a gem,
So this, my first poem, is just for them!

Joshua Rogan (4)
Little Friends Preschool, Banbridge

# My First Poem

My name is Finn and I go to preschool,
My best friend is Michael, who is really cool.
I watch PAW Patrol on TV,
Playing on my Xbox is lots of fun for me.
I just love tuna sandwiches to eat,
And sometimes ice cream for a treat.
Blue is a colour I like a lot,
My scooter is the best present I ever got.
My favourite person is Daddy, who is a gem,
So this, my first poem, is just for them!

Finn Mark Dillon (4)
Little Friends Preschool, Banbridge

# My First Poem

My name is Dylan and I go to preschool,
My best friend is Joshua, who is really cool.
I watch Peppa Pig on TV,
Playing and chasing is lots of fun for me.
I just love carrots to eat,
And sometimes Milky Ways for a treat.
Green is a colour I like a lot,
My dinosaur Rex is the best present I ever got.
My favourite person is Mummy, who is a gem,
So this, my first poem, is just for them!

Dylan Rogan (4)
Little Friends Preschool, Banbridge

# My First Poem

My name is Peter and I go to preschool,
My best friend is Luke, who is really cool.
I watch CBeebies on TV,
Playing football is lots of fun for me.
I just love jam sandwiches to eat,
And sometimes get ice cream for a treat.
Green is a colour I like a lot,
My Angry Birds Jenga is the best present I ever got.
My favourite person is my mum, who is a gem,
So this, my first poem, is just for them!

Peter McCordick (4)
Little Friends Preschool, Banbridge

# My First Poem

My name is Aimee and I go to preschool,
My best friend is Dexter, who is really cool.
I watch Curious George on TV,
Playing on my bike is lots of fun for me.
I just love sausage rolls to eat,
And sometimes chocolate for a treat.
Pink is a colour I like a lot,
My scooter is the best present I ever got.
My favourite person is my daddy, who is a gem,
So this, my first poem, is just for them!

Aimee Sneddon (4)
Little Friends Preschool, Banbridge

# My First Poem

My name is Jamie and I go to preschool,
My best friend is Jack, who is really cool.
I watch Thomas and Friends and Fireman Sam on TV,
Playing in the sand at school is lots of fun for me.
I just love turkey dinosaurs to eat,
And sometimes crisps for a treat.
Blue is a colour I like a lot,
My Ocean Rescue Centre is the best present I ever got.
My favourite person is Mummy, who is a gem,
So this, my first poem, is just for them!

Jamie McKnight (4)
Little Friends Preschool, Banbridge

# My First Poem

My name is Jack and I go to preschool,
My best friend is Jamie, who is really cool.
I watch Fireman Sam on TV,
Playing hide-and-seek is lots of fun for me.
I just love ham sandwiches to eat,
And sometimes an ice lolly for a treat.
Red is a colour I like a lot,
My fire engine is the best present I ever got.
My favourite person is my daddy, who is a gem,
So this, my first poem, is just for them!

Jack Sinnamon (4)
Little Friends Preschool, Banbridge

# My First Poem

My name is Vlad and I go to preschool,
My best friend is Daniel, who is really cool.
I watch Mickey Mouse on TV,
Playing with my trains is lots of fun for me.
I just love bananas and oranges to eat,
And sometimes my sweeties for a treat.
Yellow is a colour I like a lot,
My Santa present is the best present I ever got.
My favourite person is my mummy, who is a gem,
So this, my first poem, is just for them!

Vlad Tudor (3)
Little Rays Day Nursery, Ballymena

# My First Poem

My name is Poppy and I go to preschool,
My best friend is Kate, who is really cool.
I watch Peppa Pig on TV,
Playing with play dough is lots of fun for me.
I just love bananas to eat,
And sometimes ice cream for a treat.
Pink is a colour I like a lot,
My baby is the best present I ever got.
My favourite person is Georgie, who is a gem,
So this, my first poem, is just for them!

Poppy Drummond (4)
Little Rays Day Nursery, Ballymena

# My First Poem

My name is Pippa and I go to preschool,
My best friend is Kate, who is really cool.
I watch Peppa Pig on TV,
Playing with Peppa Pig is lots of fun for me.
I just love oranges to eat,
And sometimes popcorn for a treat.
Purple is a colour I like a lot,
My pink bear is the best present I ever got.
My favourite person is Mummy, who is a gem,
So this, my first poem, is just for them!

Pippa Drummond (4)
Little Rays Day Nursery, Ballymena

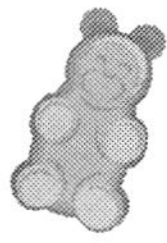

# My First Poem

My name is Daniel and I go to preschool,
My best friend is Daniel, who is really cool.
I watch Tom and Jerry on TV,
Playing Fireman Sam is lots of fun for me.
I just love apples to eat,
And sometimes a sweetie for a treat.
Red is a colour I like a lot,
My Tom and Jerry toy is the best present I ever got.
My favourite person is Sebastian, who is a gem,
So this, my first poem, is just for them!

Daniel Biegacz (4)
Little Rays Day Nursery, Ballymena

# My First Poem

My name is Lucy and I go to preschool,
My best friend is Eden, who is really cool.
I watch Frozen on TV,
Playing musical statues is lots of fun for me.
I just love pizza to eat,
And sometimes lollipops for a treat.
Pink is a colour I like a lot,
My Frozen Elsa doll is the best present I ever got.
My favourite person is Ruby, who is a gem,
So this, my first poem, is just for them!

Lucy Black (3)
Little Rays Day Nursery, Ballymena

# My First Poem

My name is Kate and I go to preschool,
My best friend is Eden, who is really cool.
I watch Peppa Pig on TV,
Playing duck duck goose is lots of fun for me.
I just love watermelon to eat,
And sometimes ice lollies for a treat.
Purple is a colour I like a lot,
My Rapunzel dress is the best present I ever got.
My favourite person is Grace, who is a gem,
So this, my first poem, is just for them!

Kate Davison (4)
Little Rays Day Nursery, Ballymena

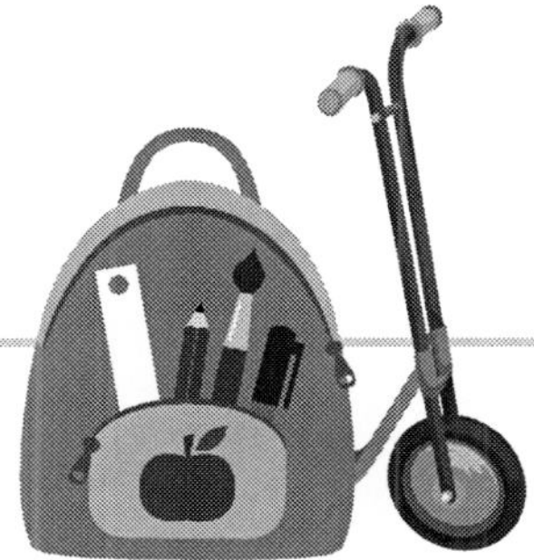

# My First Poem

My name is Jamie and I go to preschool,
My best friend is Daniel, who is really cool.
I watch SpongeBob on TV,
Playing with my fire engine is lots of fun for me.
I just love Weetabix to eat,
And sometimes an orange sweetie for a treat.
Orange is a colour I like a lot,
My computer is the best present I ever got.
My favourite person is Daniel, who is a gem,
So this, my first poem, is just for them!

Jamie Goligher (3)
Little Rays Day Nursery, Ballymena

# My First Poem

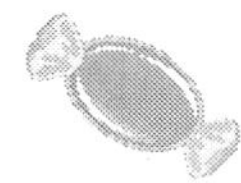

My name is Adam and I go to preschool,
My best friend is Joshua, who is really cool.
I watch dinosaurs on TV,
Playing Mario is lots of fun for me.
I just love pasta to eat,
And sometimes chocolate for a treat.
Yellow is a colour I like a lot,
My dinosaur is the best present I ever got.
My favourite person is Mummy, who is a gem,
So this, my first poem, is just for them!

Adam-Jackson Rea (4)
Little Rays Day Nursery, Ballymena

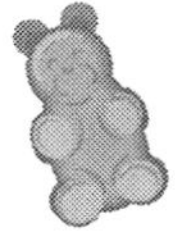

# My First Poem

My name is Lauren and I go to preschool,
My best friend is Georgie, who is really cool.
I watch Rapunzel on TV,
Playing with my Elsa doll is lots of fun for me.
I just love Nutella on toast to eat,
And sometimes a Barney Bear for a treat.
Light purple is a colour I like a lot,
My Frozen doll is the best present I ever got.
My favourite person is my mummy, who is a gem,
So this, my first poem, is just for them!

Lauren Rose Mooney (4)
Little Rays Day Nursery, Ballymena

# My First Poem

My name is Kendal and I go to preschool,
My best friend is Lauren, who is really cool.
I watch Peppa Pig on TV,
Playing duck duck goose is lots of fun for me.
I just love pasta to eat,
And sometimes biscuits and jaffa cakes for a treat.
Pink is a colour I like a lot,
My Elsa doll is the best present I ever got.
My favourite person is my mummy, who is a gem,
So this, my first poem, is just for them!

Kendal Conway (4)
Little Rays Day Nursery, Ballymena

# My First Poem

My name is Daniel and I go to preschool,
My best friend is Oran, who is really cool.
I watch Frozen on TV,
Playing with rally cars is lots of fun for me.
I just love a sandwich to eat,
And sometimes biscuits for a treat.
Green is a colour I like a lot,
My rally car is the best present I ever got.
My favourite person is Daddy, who is a gem,
So this, my first poem, is just for them!

Daniel Mullan (3)
Little Rays Day Nursery, Ballymena

# My First Poem

My name is Ella and I go to preschool,
My best friend is Daniel, who is really cool.
I watch Frozen on TV,
Playing with my Elsa doll is lots of fun for me.
I just love strawberries to eat,
And sometimes sweeties for a treat.
Pink is a colour I like a lot,
My Elsa doll is the best present I ever got.
My favourite person is Daniel, who is a gem,
So this, my first poem, is just for them!

Ella Tweed (3)
Little Rays Day Nursery, Ballymena

# My First Poem

My name is Michael and I go to preschool,
My best friend is Tom, who is really cool.
I watch Power Rangers on TV,
Playing football is lots of fun for me.
I just love lasagne to eat,
And sometimes Smarties for a treat.
Silver is a colour I like a lot,
My go-kart is the best present I ever got.
My favourite person is Mum, who is a gem,
So this, my first poem, is just for them!

Michael Gallagher (4)
Little Rays Day Nursery, Ballymena

# My First Poem

My name is Harry and I go to preschool,
My best friend is Marco, who is really cool.
I watch Frozen on TV,
Playing with tractors is lots of fun for me.
I just love spaghetti to eat,
And sometimes brown chocolate for a treat.
Orange is a colour I like a lot,
My Baymax is the best present I ever got.
My favourite person is Daddy, who is a gem,
So this, my first poem, is just for them!

Harry Bingham (3)
Little Rays Day Nursery, Ballymena

# My First Poem

My name is Tom and I go to preschool,
My best friend is Michael, who is really cool.
I watch CBeebies on TV,
Playing horses is lots of fun for me.
I just love tomatoes and sauce to eat,
And sometimes Milky Bars for a treat.
Red is a colour I like a lot,
My Power Ranger is the best present I ever got.
My favourite person is Danni, who is a gem,
So this, my first poem, is just for them!

Tom McAuley (3)
Little Rays Day Nursery, Ballymena

# My First Poem

My name is Cameron and I go to preschool,
My best friend is Mummy, who is really cool.
I watch the Moshi Monster movie on TV,
Playing hide-and-seek with Mummy and Nelly
is lots of fun for me.
I just love Happy Meals at McDonald's to eat,
And sometimes chocolate bars for a treat.
Orange is a colour I like a lot,
My lorry is the best present I ever got.
My favourite person is Mummy, who is a gem,
So this, my first poem, is just for them!

Cameron Ward (3)
Little Rays Day Nursery, Ballymena

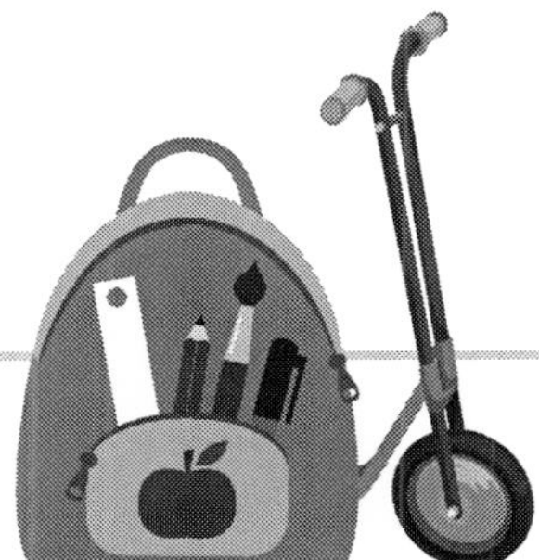

# My First Poem

My name is Oran and I go to preschool,
My best friend is Jamie, who is really cool.
I watch Star Wars on TV,
Playing Candy Crush is lots of fun for me.
I just love a banana to eat,
And sometimes a wee bun for a treat.
Green is a colour I like a lot,
My brown teddy bear is the best present I ever got.
My favourite person is Daniel, who is a gem,
So this, my first poem, is just for them!

Oran McAfee (3)
Little Rays Day Nursery, Ballymena

# My First Poem

My name is Shéa and I go to preschool,
My best friend is Coby, who is really cool.
I watch Power Rangers on TV,
Playing with dinosaurs and sheep is lots of fun for me.
I just love burgers to eat,
And sometimes ice cream for a treat.
Green is a colour I like a lot,
My sword is the best present I ever got.
My favourite person is Mummy, who is a gem,
So this, my first poem, is just for them!

Shéa Freddie George Cushenan (4)
Little Wombles Cross-Community Playgroup, Magherafelt

# My First Poem

My name is Ethan and I go to preschool,
My best friend is Kala, who is really cool.
I watch Tractor Ted and Bob the Builder on TV,
Playing on the swings and slides and with tractors is lots of fun for me.
I just love eggs, sausages and Granny's bread to eat,
And sometimes ice cream for a treat.
Green is a colour I like a lot,
My remote control digger is the best present I ever got.
My favourite person is Katie Ann, who is a gem,
So this, my first poem, is just for them!

Ethan Heron (3)
Little Wombles Cross-Community Playgroup, Magherafelt

# My First Poem

My name is Amy and I go to preschool,
My best friend is Rosie, who is really cool.
I watch Frozen on TV,
Playing with my Elsa and Anna dolls is lots of fun for me.
I just love carrots, peas, potatoes and gravy to eat,
And sometimes Oreos for a treat.
Pink is a colour I like a lot,
My Frozen dress is the best present I ever got.
My favourite person is Mary, who is a gem,
So this, my first poem, is just for them!

Amy Louise McBride (4)
Little Wombles Cross-Community Playgroup, Magherafelt

# My First Poem

My name is Kaitlyn and I go to preschool,
My best friend is Tanya, who is really cool.
I watch Peppa Pig on TV,
Playing on my DS is lots of fun for me.
I just love lasagne to eat,
And sometimes sweets for a treat.
Red is a colour I like a lot,
My tablet is the best present I ever got.
My favourite person is Mummy, who is a gem,
So this, my first poem, is just for them!

Kaitlyn Kelly (4)
Little Wombles Cross-Community Playgroup, Magherafelt

# My First Poem

My name is Kyla and I go to preschool,
My best friend is Tanya, who is really cool.
I watch Ben and Holly on TV,
Playing stuck in the mud is lots of fun for me.
I just love chicken nuggets to eat,
And sometimes ice lollies for a treat.
Purple is a colour I like a lot,
My Baby Annabell is the best present I ever got.
My favourite person is Mummy, who is a gem,
So this, my first poem, is just for them!

Kyla Kelly (4)
Little Wombles Cross-Community Playgroup, Magherafelt

# My First Poem

My name is Charlie and I go to preschool,
My best friend is Callum, who is really cool.
I watch Mr Tumble on TV,
Playing shopping lists is lots of fun for me.
I just love pasta and strawberries to eat,
And sometimes chocolate for a treat.
Purple is a colour I like a lot,
My bike is the best present I ever got.
My favourite person is Daddy, who is a gem,
So this, my first poem, is just for them!

Charlotte McGuffin (3)
Maylands Nursery, St Saviours

# My First Poem

My name is Emily and I go to preschool,
My best friend is Libby, who is really cool.
I watch Melody on TV,
Playing with my friends and cousins is lots of fun for me.
I just love sausages to eat,
And sometimes pink ice cream with sprinkles for a treat.
Pink is a colour I like a lot,
My ducky is the best present I ever got.
My favourite person is Daddy, who is a gem,
So this, my first poem, is just for them!

Emily Louise Ozanne (2)
Maylands Nursery, St Saviours

# My First Poem

My name is Lottie and I go to preschool,
My best friend is Samuel, who is really cool.
I watch Peppa Pig on TV,
Playing on my swing is lots of fun for me.
I just love Daddy's bread (baguette) to eat,
And sometimes sausages and chips for a treat.
Pink is a colour I like a lot,
My pink scooter is the best present I ever got.
My favourite person is Granny, who is a gem,
So this, my first poem, is just for them!

Lottie Holland (2)
Maylands Nursery, St Saviours

# My First Poem

My name is Sukie and I go to preschool,
My best friend is Jay Jay, my big brother, who is really cool.
I watch Peppa Pig on TV,
Playing with Play-Doh is lots of fun for me.
I just love blueberries to eat,
And sometimes chocolate for a treat.
Yellow is a colour I like a lot,
My trampoline is the best present I ever got.
My favourite person is Nana, who is a gem,
So this, my first poem, is just for them!

Sukie Lynne Allsopp (2)
Maylands Nursery, St Saviours

# My First Poem

My name is Florence and I go to preschool,
My best friend is Gregory, who is really cool.
I watch Peppa Pig on TV,
Playing ball around the circle is lots of fun for me.
I just love fish and chips to eat,
And sometimes a cow biscuit for a treat.
Yellow is a colour I like a lot,
My Bub Bub is the best present I ever got.
My favourite person is Jakey, who is a gem,
So this, my first poem, is just for them!

Florence Emily Hazell (3)
Maylands Nursery, St Saviours

# My First Poem

My name is Callum and I go to preschool,
My best friend is Robyn, who is really cool.
I watch Thomas the Tank Engine on TV,
Playing with my toys is lots of fun for me.
I just love pasta to eat,
And sometimes pizza for a treat.
Orange is a colour I like a lot,
My Play-Doh is the best present I ever got.
My favourite person is Cameron, who is a gem,
So this, my first poem, is just for them!

Callum Slane (3)
Maylands Nursery, St Saviours

# My First Poem

My name is Elsa and I go to preschool,
My best friend is Florence, who is really cool.
I watch Frozen on TV,
Playing and dancing is lots of fun for me.
I just love owl ice cream to eat,
And sometimes scrambled snake for a treat.
Purple is a colour I like a lot,
My farm is the best present I ever got.
My favourite person is Mummy, who is a gem,
So this, my first poem, is just for them!

Elsa Bisson (2)
Maylands Nursery, St Saviours

# My First Poem

My name is Joel and I go to preschool,
My best friend is Jack, who is really cool.
I watch Shaun the Sheep on TV,
Playing with tractors is lots of fun for me.
I just love sausages and red sauce to eat,
And sometimes I get lollipops for a treat.
Red is a colour I like a lot,
My scooter is the best present I ever got.
My favourite person is Granny, who is a gem,
So this, my first poem, is just for them!

Joel Jamieson (3)
Mother Goose Playgroup, Ballycastle

# My First Poem

My name is Freya and I go to preschool,
My best friend is Erin, who is really cool.
I watch Elsa on TV,
Playing with the ponies is lots of fun for me.
I just love apples to eat,
And sometimes sweeties for a treat.
Pink is a colour I like a lot,
My Rainbow Dash pony is the best present I ever got.
My favourite person is Mummy, who is a gem,
So this, my first poem, is just for them!

Freya Bougourd (3)
Preschool Duval, Guernsey

# My First Poem

My name is Kaylan and I go to preschool,
My best friend is Joseph, who is really cool.
I watch Thomas the Tank Engine on TV,
Playing and reading stories is lots of fun for me.
I just love sausages to eat,
And sometimes chips for a treat.
Pink is a colour I like a lot,
My Thomas engine is the best present I ever got.
My favourite person is Daddy, who is a gem,
So this, my first poem, is just for them!

Kaylan Gaudion (3)
Preschool Duval, Guernsey

# My First Poem

My name is Erin and I go to preschool,
My best friend is Freya, who is really cool.
I watch PAW Patrol on TV,
Playing with dinosaurs is lots of fun for me.
I just love fish fingers to eat,
And sometimes chocolate buttons for a treat.
Green is a colour I like a lot,
My dinosaur choo choo train is the best present
I ever got.
My favourite person is Freya, who is a gem,
So this, my first poem, is just for them!

Erin De Garis (4)
Preschool Duval, Guernsey

# My First Poem

My name is Aurelia and I go to preschool,
My best friend is Lucy, who is really cool.
I watch Frozen on TV,
Playing with puzzles is lots of fun for me.
I just love chicken to eat,
And sometimes chocolate for a treat.
Red is a colour I like a lot,
My boat is the best present I ever got.
My favourite person is Mummy, who is a gem,
So this, my first poem, is just for them!

Aurelia Simon (3)
Preschool Duval, Guernsey

# My First Poem

My name is Max and I go to preschool,
My best friend is my dad, who is really cool.
I watch Minnie Mouse and Aladdin on TV,
Playing with tractors is lots of fun for me.
I just love pasta to eat,
And sometimes chocolate, sweets and ice cream for a treat.
Blue is a colour I like a lot,
My tractor is the best present I ever got.
My favourite person is Daddy, who is a gem,
So this, my first poem, is just for them!

Max David Corbet (3)
Preschool Duval, Guernsey

# My First Poem

My name is Finlay and I go to preschool,
My best friend is Amy, who is really cool.
I watch Peppa Pig on TV,
Playing with cars is lots of fun for me.
I just love chocolate to eat,
And sometimes a chocolate brownie for a treat.
Green is a colour I like a lot,
My ambulance is the best present I ever got.
My favourite person is Morley, who is a gem,
So this, my first poem, is just for them!

Finlay Brown (3)
Preschool Duval, Guernsey

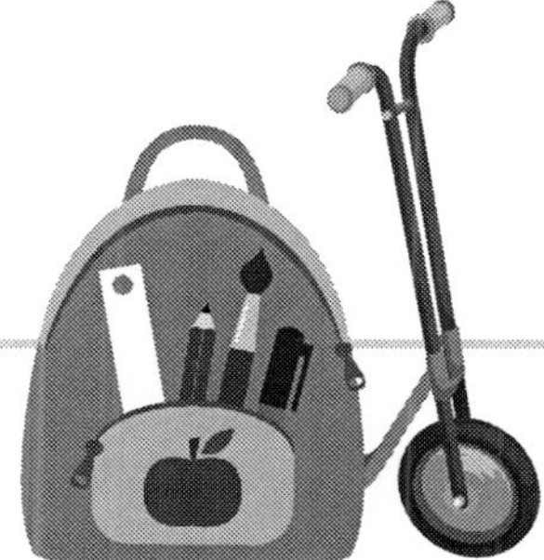

# My First Poem

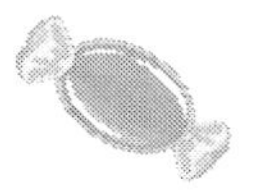

My name is Noah and I go to preschool,
My best friend is Toby, my dog, who is really cool.
I watch Gruffalo's Child on TV,
Playing Minecraft is lots of fun for me.
I just love tomatoes to eat,
And sometimes ice cream for a treat.
Blue is a colour I like a lot,
My DS is the best present I ever got.
My favourite person is Jake, who is a gem,
So this, my first poem, is just for them!

Noah Van Der Linden (4)
Preschool Duval, Guernsey

# My First Poem

My name is Ava and I go to preschool,
My best friend is Noah, who is really cool.
I watch PAW Patrol on TV,
Playing Rubble on the Double is lots of fun for me.
I just love Smiley Faces and bread to eat,
And sometimes lollipops and Kinder eggs for a treat.
Pink is a colour I like a lot,
My doll is the best present I ever got.
My favourite person is Daddy, who is a gem,
So this, my first poem, is just for them!

Ava De La Mare (3)
Preschool Duval, Guernsey

# My First Poem

My name is Amelia and I go to preschool,
My best friend is Sophia, who is really cool.
I watch Frozen on TV,
Playing with Steve, my tiger is lots of fun for me.
I just love cookies to eat,
And sometimes chocolate fingers for a treat.
Red is a colour I like a lot,
My helicopter that has a hook to save the baby animals is the best present I ever got.
My favourite person is Gran, who is a gem,
So this, my first poem, is just for them!

Amelia Bichard (4)
Preschool Duval, Guernsey

# My First Poem

My name is Tallulah and I go to preschool,
My best friend is Kiriana, who is really cool.
I watch Peter Rabbit and Scooby-Doo on TV,
Playing with my teddy with a Christmas hat on is lots of fun for me.
I just love ham to eat,
And sometimes cake for a treat.
Pink is a colour I like a lot,
My Frozen dress is the best present I ever got.
My favourite person is Mummy, who is a gem,
So this, my first poem, is just for them!

Tallulah Hutchison (3)
Preschool Duval, Guernsey

# My First Poem

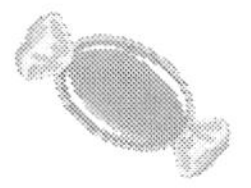

My name is Sophie and I go to preschool,
My best friend is Sophie R, who is really cool.
I watch Frozen on TV,
Playing with my dolls is lots of fun for me.
I just love a Cheestring to eat,
And sometimes an ice lolly for a treat.
Pink is a colour I like a lot,
My Peppa Pig cake is the best present I ever got.
My favourite person is Lucy, who is a gem,
So this, my first poem, is just for them!

Sophie Dawn Baker (3)
Preschool Duval, Guernsey

# My First Poem

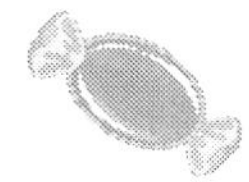

My name is Sophie and I go to preschool,
My best friend is Lucy, who is really cool.
I watch Peppa Pig on TV,
Playing with Lucy is lots of fun for me.
I just love cheese sandwiches to eat,
And sometimes sweets for a treat.
Pink is a colour I like a lot,
My big doll is the best present I ever got.
My favourite person is Mummy, who is a gem,
So this, my first poem, is just for them!

Sophie Grace Louise Ridges (3)
Preschool Duval, Guernsey

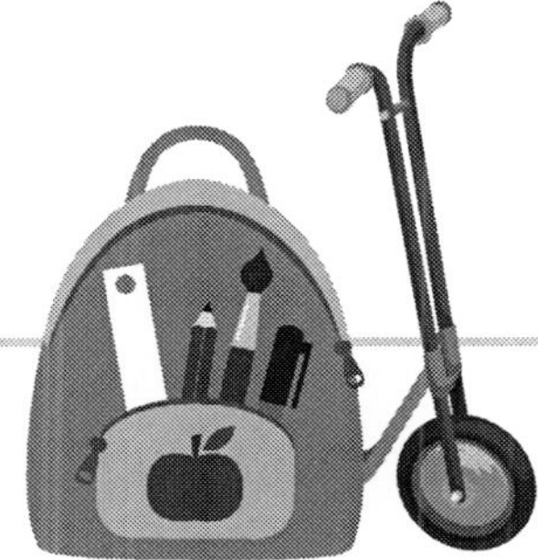

# My First Poem

My name is Lucy and I go to preschool,
My best friend is Sophie, who is really cool.
I watch Frozen on TV,
Playing with Sophie is lots of fun for me.
I just love apples to eat,
And sometimes sweeties for a treat.
Pink is a colour I like a lot,
My Frozen book is the best present I ever got.
My favourite person is Sophie, who is a gem,
So this, my first poem, is just for them!

Lucy Oregan (4)
Preschool Duval, Guernsey

# My First Poem

My name is Archie and I go to preschool,
My best friend is Tenzin, who is really cool.
I watch Postman Pat on TV,
Playing with jigsaw puzzles is lots of fun for me.
I just love crisps to eat,
And sometimes ice cream for a treat.
Green is a colour I like a lot,
My car is the best present I ever got.
My favourite person is Mummy, who is a gem,
So this, my first poem, is just for them!

Archie Michael Robins (2)
Preschool Duval, Guernsey

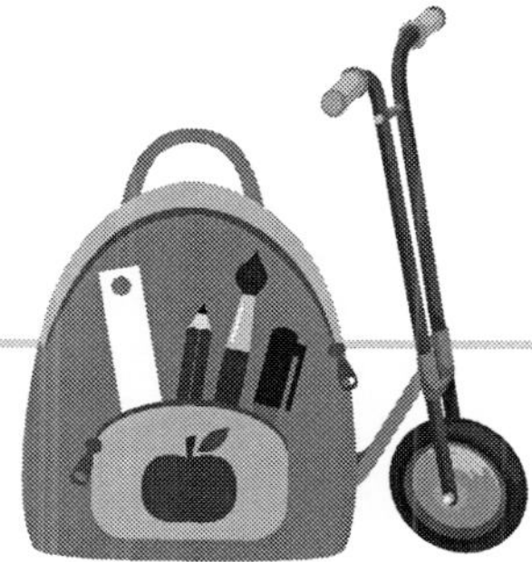

# My First Poem

My name is Connor and I go to preschool,
My best friend is Harry, who is really cool.
I watch Peppa Pig on TV,
Playing with Thomas the Tank Engine is lots of fun for me.
I just love carrots to eat,
And sometimes cake for a treat.
Red is a colour I like a lot,
My cave is the best present I ever got.
My favourite person is Mummy, who is a gem,
So this, my first poem, is just for them!

Connor De Carteret (3)
Preschool Duval, Guernsey

# My First Poem

My name is Amy and I go to preschool,
My best friend is Finlay, who is really cool.
I watch Sofia the First on TV,
Playing with the fairies is lots of fun for me.
I just love chocolate cake to eat,
And sometimes chocolate for a treat.
Purple is a colour I like a lot,
My Elsa dress is the best present I ever got.
My favourite person is my cousin, Maisy, who is a gem,
So this, my first poem, is just for them!

Amy Tersigni (4)
Preschool Duval, Guernsey

# My First Poem

My name is Flynn and I go to preschool,
My best friend is Holly, who is really cool.
I watch superheroes on TV,
Playing with Hot Wheels is lots of fun for me.
I just love cheesy pasta in the red box to eat,
And sometimes chocolate for a treat.
Green is a colour I like a lot,
My Spider-Man is the best present I ever got.
My favourite person is Daddy, who is a gem,
So this, my first poem, is just for them!

Flynn Campbell Muir (4)
Preschool Duval, Guernsey

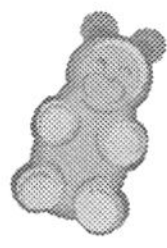

# My First Poem

My name is Isabelle and I go to preschool,
My best friend is Chloe, who is really cool.
I watch The Furchester Hotel on TV,
Playing with my toys is lots of fun for me.
I just love chips to eat,
And sometimes yoghurt for a treat.
Pink is a colour I like a lot,
My Shopkins is the best present I ever got.
My favourite person is Chloe, who is a gem,
So this, my first poem, is just for them!

Isabelle Beale (3)
Preschool Duval, Guernsey

# My First Poem

My name is Phoebe and I go to preschool,
My best friend is Sophia, who is really cool.
I watch Puffin Rock on TV,
Playing Lego is lots of fun for me.
I just love pasta to eat,
And sometimes a Kinder egg for a treat.
Pink is a colour I like a lot,
My birdie is the best present I ever got.
My favourite person is Daddy, who is a gem,
So this, my first poem, is just for them!

Phoebe Jones (4)
Preschool Duval, Guernsey

# My First Poem

My name is Morley and I go to preschool,
My best friend is Little Grace, who is really cool.
I watch Frozen on TV,
Playing with Playmobil is lots of fun for me.
I just love baguettes to eat,
And sometimes chocolate for a treat.
Blue is a colour I like a lot,
My space toy is the best present I ever got.
My favourite person is Little Grace, who is a gem,
So this, my first poem, is just for them!

Morley Tostevin (3)
Preschool Duval, Guernsey

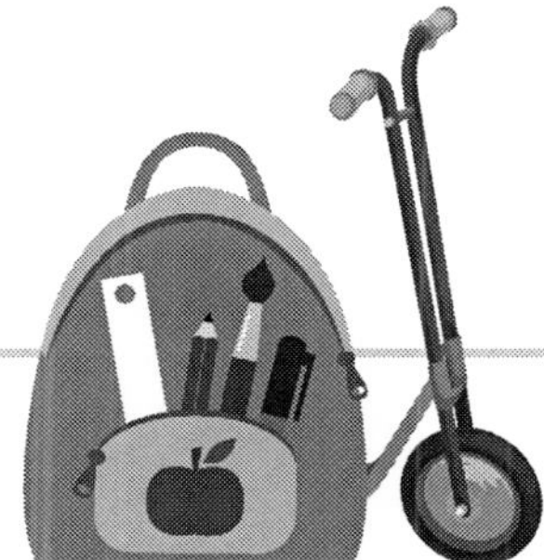

# My First Poem

My name is Sophia and I go to preschool,
My best friend is Devon, who is really cool.
I watch Peppa Pig on TV,
Playing with Lego is lots of fun for me.
I just love spaghetti Bolognese to eat,
And sometimes lollipops for a treat.
Pink is a colour I like a lot,
My horse bed is the best present I ever got.
My favourite person is my Pop-Pop, who is a gem,
So this, my first poem, is just for them!

Sophia Hope Le Brun (4)
Preschool Duval, Guernsey

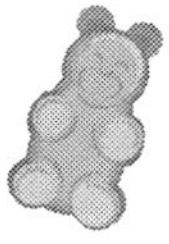

# My First Poem

My name is Carragh-Louise and I go to preschool,
My best friend is Sofia, who is really cool.
I watch Peppa Pig and Disney princesses on TV,
Playing with my Barbie dolls is lots of fun for me.
I just love sausages and chicken nuggets to eat,
And sometimes I have ice cream for a treat.
Pink is a colour I like a lot,
My trip to Disneyland is the best present I ever got.
My favourite person is Daddy Lee, who is a gem,
So this, my first poem, is just for them!

Carragh-Louise Nicholas (4)
St Joseph's Community Playgroup, Londonderry

# My First Poem

My name is Cein and I go to preschool,
My best friend is Rhys, who is really cool.
I watch Spider-Man and Power Rangers on TV,
Playing dress-up is lots of fun for me.
I just love potato bread to eat,
And sometimes ice cream for a treat.
Blue is a colour I like a lot,
My red motorbike is the best present I ever got.
My favourite person is Spider-Man, who is a gem,
So this, my first poem, is just for them!

Cein Hume (3)
St Joseph's Community Playgroup, Londonderry

# My First Poem

My name is Rhys and I go to preschool,
My best friend is Cein, who is really cool.
I watch Scooby-Doo on TV,
Playing with my turtles is lots of fun for me.
I just love pasta and cheese to eat,
And sometimes a Kinder Surprise for a treat.
Red is a colour I like a lot,
My red motorbike is the best present I ever got.
My favourite person is The Flash, who is a gem,
So this, my first poem, is just for them!

Rhys Hume (3)
St Joseph's Community Playgroup, Londonderry

# My First Poem

My name is Brooke and I go to preschool,
My best friend is Ella, who is really cool.
I watch Peppa Pig on TV,
Playing with play dough is lots of fun for me.
I just love pasta to eat,
And sometimes chocolate for a treat.
Purple is a colour I like a lot,
My electric motorbike is the best present I ever got.
My favourite person is Nanny, who is a gem,
So this, my first poem, is just for them!

Brooke Riona Scanlon Whoriskey (4)
St Joseph's Community Playgroup, Londonderry

# My First Poem

My name is Ella and I go to preschool,
My best friend is Brooke, who is really cool.
I watch Chloe's Closet on TV,
Playing outside is lots of fun for me.
I just love noodles to eat,
And sometimes ice cream for a treat.
Red is a colour I like a lot,
My bike is the best present I ever got.
My favourite person is Fionn, who is a gem,
So this, my first poem, is just for them!

Ella Johnson (4)
St Joseph's Community Playgroup, Londonderry

# My First Poem

My name is Maisie and I go to preschool,
My best friend is Roisin, who is really cool.
I watch SpongeBob on TV,
Playing with my black Stormtrooper and doll's house is lots of fun for me.
I just love fish cakes and mash to eat,
And sometimes I have ice pops and biscuits for a treat.
Pink is a colour I like a lot,
My R2D2 is the best present I ever got.
My favourite person is my mummy, who is a gem,
So this, my first poem, is just for them!

Maisie Lock (4)
St Joseph's Community Playgroup, Londonderry

# My First Poem

My name is Donncha and I go to preschool,
My best friend is Maddison, who is really cool.
I watch Ninja Turtles on TV,
Playing kitchens is lots of fun for me.
I just love ham, cheese and pancakes to eat,
And sometimes a Kinder bar for a treat.
Red is a colour I like a lot,
My Batman house is the best present I ever got.
My favourite person is Daddy, who is a gem,
So this, my first poem, is just for them!

Donncha Corry (4)
St Mary's Preschool Centre, Strabane

# My First Poem

My name is Ben and I go to preschool,
My best friend is Blaine, who is really cool.
I watch My Little Pony on TV,
Playing with my Spider-Man helicopter is lots of fun for me.
I just love pasta to eat,
And sometimes ice cream for a treat.
Blue is a colour I like a lot,
My toy truck is the best present I ever got.
My favourite person is my sister, Sophie, who is a gem,
So this, my first poem, is just for them!

Ben Devine (4)
St Mary's Preschool Centre, Strabane

# My First Poem

My name is Aidan and I go to preschool,
My best friend is Fionn, who is really cool.
I watch Ninja Turtles on TV,
Playing on my bike is lots of fun for me.
I just love pasta to eat,
And sometimes yoghurt for a treat.
Red is a colour I like a lot,
My fire engine is the best present I ever got.
My favourite person is Mummy, who is a gem,
So this, my first poem, is just for them!

Aidan Parker (4)
St Mary's Preschool Centre, Strabane

# My First Poem

My name is Shay and I go to preschool,
My best friend is Noah, who is really cool.
I watch Ninja Turtles on TV,
Playing with my cousin, Noah is lots of fun for me.
I just love pasta to eat,
And sometimes chocolate for a treat.
Red is a colour I like a lot,
My Ninja Turtle from Santa is the best present I ever got.
My favourite person is Daddy, who is a gem,
So this, my first poem, is just for them!

Shay Gallagher (4)
St Mary's Preschool Centre, Strabane

# My First Poem

My name is Anthony and I go to preschool,
My best friend is John Paul, who is really cool.
I watch Lightning McQueen on TV,
Playing races around the table is lots of fun for me.
I just love roasties to eat,
And sometimes biscuits for a treat.
Red is a colour I like a lot,
My big Lightning McQueen car is the best present I ever got.
My favourite person is John Paul, who is a gem,
So this, my first poem, is just for them!

Anthony McClafferty (3)
St Paul's Nursery School, Belfast

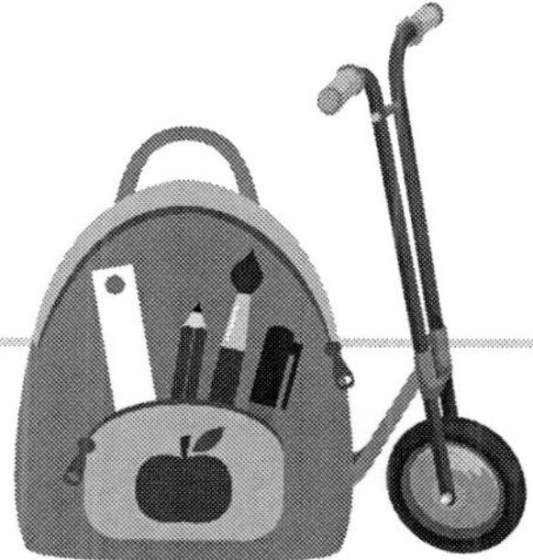

# My First Poem

My name is Jayden and I go to preschool,
My best friend is Shea, who is really cool.
I watch Fireman Sam on TV,
Playing football is lots of fun for me.
I just love veggies to eat,
And sometimes sweets for a treat.
Blue is a colour I like a lot,
My Innotab is the best present I ever got.
My favourite person is Mummy, who is a gem,
So this, my first poem, is just for them!

Jayden McShane (4)
St Paul's Nursery School, Belfast

# My First Poem

My name is Orlaith and I go to preschool,
My best friend is Ruby, who is really cool.
I watch cartoons on TV,
Playing games is lots of fun for me.
I just love pizza to eat,
And sometimes ice cream for a treat.
Purple is a colour I like a lot,
My iPad is the best present I ever got.
My favourite person is my mummy, who is a gem,
So this, my first poem, is just for them!

Orlaith McShane (4)
St Paul's Nursery School, Belfast

# My First Poem

My name is Daniel and I go to preschool,
My best friend is my cousin, Iris, who is really cool.
I watch Team Umizoomi on TV,
Playing Lego with Daddy is lots of fun for me.
I just love Cheerios to eat,
And sometimes chocolate cake for a treat.
Orange is a colour I like a lot,
My Ocean Rescue Centre is the best present I ever got.
My favourite person is Dinky, who is a gem,
So this, my first poem, is just for them!

Daniel Morgan (4)
St Paul's Nursery School, Belfast

# My First Poem

My name is Shea and I go to preschool,
My best friend is Anton, who is really cool.
I watch Snow White and the Seven Dwarfs on TV,
Playing on my scooter is lots of fun for me.
I just love pie to eat,
And sometimes lollipops and crisps for a treat.
Light blue is a colour I like a lot,
My fire engine is the best present I ever got.
My favourite person is Uncle Joe, who is a gem,
So this, my first poem, is just for them!

Shea McMenamy (3)
St Paul's Nursery School, Belfast

# My First Poem

My name is Cora and I go to preschool,
My best friend is Aaliyah, who is really cool.
I watch Team Umizoomi on TV,
Playing with my snakes is lots of fun for me.
I just love apples to eat,
And sometimes buns for a treat.
Pink is a colour I like a lot,
My spider, Sandy is the best present I ever got.
My favourite person is my mummy, who is a gem,
So this, my first poem, is just for them!

Cora Heaney McGlone (3)
St Paul's Nursery School, Belfast

# My First Poem

My name is Aaliyah and I go to preschool,
My best friend is Cora, who is really cool.
I watch cartoons on TV,
Playing with building blocks is lots of fun for me.
I just love grapes to eat,
And sometimes chocolate ice cream for a treat.
Red is a colour I like a lot,
My Elsa doll is the best present I ever got.
My favourite person is Mummy, Marianne, who is a gem,
So this, my first poem, is just for them!

Aaliyah Nicole Dy (3)
St Paul's Nursery School, Belfast

# My First Poem

My name is Ethan and I go to preschool,
My best friend is Anthony, who is really cool.
I watch Spider-Man on TV,
Playing with my cousin, Ava is lots of fun for me.
I just love having a burger to eat,
And sometimes a lollipop for a treat.
Blue is a colour I like a lot,
My Batman figure is the best present I ever got.
My favourite person is my uncle Ciaran, who is a gem,
So this, my first poem, is just for them!

Ethan Patrick Hall (3)
St Paul's Nursery School, Belfast

# My First Poem

My name is Olivia and I go to preschool,
My best friend is Orlaith, who is really cool.
I watch Peppa Pig on TV,
Playing with my cousin, Ava is lots of fun for me.
I just love having potatoes to eat,
And sometimes a Kinder egg for a treat.
Purple is a colour I like a lot,
My Anna from Frozen doll is the best present I ever got.
My favourite person is Daddy, who is a gem,
So this, my first poem, is just for them!

Olivia Rose Hall (3)
St Paul's Nursery School, Belfast

# My First Poem

My name is Caoimhin and I go to preschool,
My best friend is Max, who is really cool.
I watch Power Rangers on TV,
Playing wrestling is lots of fun for me.
I just love mashed potatoes to eat,
And sometimes sweetie yoghurts for a treat.
Red is a colour I like a lot,
My kitchen is the best present I ever got.
My favourite person is my mummy, who is a gem,
So this, my first poem, is just for them!

Caoimhin Boyle-McCrudden (4)
St Paul's Nursery School, Belfast

# My First Poem

My name is Aoife and I go to preschool,
My best friend is Spot, who is really cool.
I watch PAW Patrol on TV,
Playing dress-up is lots of fun for me.
I just love rice to eat,
And sometimes ice cream for a treat.
Purple is a colour I like a lot,
My Spot is the best present I ever got.
My favourite person is GaGa, who is a gem,
So this, my first poem, is just for them!

Aoife Clarke (4)
St Paul's Nursery School, Belfast

# My First Poem

My name is Aaron and I go to preschool,
My best friend is Dillion, who is really cool.
I watch The Simpsons on TV,
Playing football is lots of fun for me.
I just love pizza and chips to eat,
And sometimes chocolate for a treat.
Green is a colour I like a lot,
My Hurley helmet is the best present I ever got.
My favourite person is Mummy, who is a gem,
So this, my first poem, is just for them!

Aaron Turley (4)
St Paul's Nursery School, Belfast

# My First Poem

My name is Holly and I go to preschool,
My best friend is Clodagh, who is really cool.
I watch Sofia the First on TV,
Playing princesses is lots of fun for me.
I just love chips to eat,
And sometimes chocolate for a treat.
Pink is a colour I like a lot,
My Shopkins is the best present I ever got.
My favourite person is my mummy, who is a gem,
So this, my first poem, is just for them!

Holly Boyle (4)
St Paul's Nursery School, Belfast

# My First Poem

My name is Sophia and I go to preschool,
My best friend is Meabh, who is really cool.
I watch Sofia the First on TV,
Playing hide-and-seek is lots of fun for me.
I just love roast beef and carrots to eat,
And sometimes chocolate cake for a treat.
Pink is a colour I like a lot,
My Pinkie Pie Pony is the best present I ever got.
My favourite person is my mummy, who is a gem,
So this, my first poem, is just for them!

Sophia Rose Reid (4)
St Paul's Nursery School, Belfast

# My First Poem

My name is Daire and I go to preschool,
My best friend is Max, who is really cool.
I watch PAW Patrol on TV,
Playing Scooby-Doo is lots of fun for me.
I just love pizza to eat,
And sometimes chocolate for a treat.
Green is a colour I like a lot,
My Mystery Machine is the best present I ever got.
My favourite person is Mummy, who is a gem,
So this, my first poem, is just for them!

Daire Mulholland (3)
St Paul's Nursery School, Belfast

# My First Poem

My name is Teyona and I go to preschool,
My best friend is Autumn, who is really cool.
I watch Dora the Explorer on TV,
Playing magic games is lots of fun for me.
I just love vegetable soup and potatoes to eat,
And sometimes ice cream for a treat.
Purple is a colour I like a lot,
My dream house is the best present I ever got.
My favourite person is my mummy, who is a gem,
So this, my first poem, is just for them!

Teyona McKnight-Rooney (3)
St Paul's Nursery School, Belfast

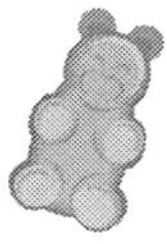

# My First Poem

My name is Lexi and I go to preschool,
My best friend is Tiona, who is really cool.
I watch Mickey Mouse on TV,
Playing hide-and-seek is lots of fun for me.
I just love tuna and pasta to eat,
And sometimes sweets for a treat.
Purple is a colour I like a lot,
My guitar is the best present I ever got.
My favourite person is Granny Maura, who is a gem,
So this, my first poem, is just for them!

Lexi Fegan McCluskey (3)
St Paul's Nursery School, Belfast

# My First Poem

My name is Ava and I go to preschool,
My best friend is Tara, who is really cool.
I watch Frozen on TV,
Playing with Mr Funny Face is lots of fun for me.
I just love sausages and chicken nuggets to eat,
And sometimes chocolate for a treat.
Yellow is a colour I like a lot,
My purple bike is the best present I ever got.
My favourite person is my mummy, who is a gem,
So this, my first poem, is just for them!

Ava Madeline Forsythe (3)
The Beeches Day Nursery, Craigavon

# My First Poem

My name is Holly and I go to preschool,
My best friend is Olivia, who is really cool.
I watch Ben and Holly on TV,
Playing with the babies and dolls is lots of fun for me.
I just love ham sandwiches to eat,
And sometimes chocolate for a treat.
Pink is a colour I like a lot,
My Frozen toy is the best present I ever got.
My favourite person is my mummy, who is a gem,
So this, my first poem, is just for them!

Holly Lily Irwin (4)
The Beeches Day Nursery, Craigavon

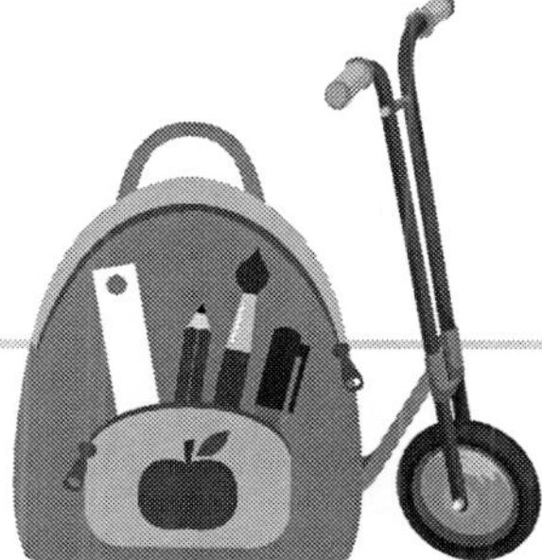

# My First Poem

My name is Dylan and I go to preschool,
My best friend is Conor, who is really cool.
I watch Toy Story on TV,
Playing football is lots of fun for me.
I just love sausage rolls and jelly to eat,
And sometimes sweets for a treat.
Red is a colour I like a lot,
My fire station is the best present I ever got.
My favourite person is Daddy, who is a gem,
So this, my first poem, is just for them!

Dylan Moore (3)
The Beeches Day Nursery, Craigavon

# My First Poem

My name is Adam and I go to preschool,
My best friend is Nathan, who is really cool.
I watch Hiccup on TV,
Playing superheroes is lots of fun for me.
I just love spaghetti Bolognese to eat,
And sometimes a fudge for a treat.
Blue is a colour I like a lot,
My Spider-Man is the best present I ever got.
My favourite person is Daddy, who is a gem,
So this, my first poem, is just for them!

Adam McCorry (4)
The Beeches Day Nursery, Craigavon

# My First Poem

My name is Codey and I go to preschool,
My best friend is Korbin, who is really cool.
I watch Mickey Mouse on TV,
Playing Buzz Lightyear and Woody is lots of fun for me.
I just love muffins to eat,
And sometimes chewy sweets for a treat.
Red is a colour I like a lot,
My Slinky dog is the best present I ever got.
My favourite person is my brother, Korbin, who is a gem,
So this, my first poem, is just for them!

Codey Malcolm (4)
The Beeches Day Nursery, Craigavon

# My First Poem

My name is Emilia and I go to preschool,
My best friend is George, who is really cool.
I watch Dora and Peppa Pig on TV,
Playing with my dolls is lots of fun for me.
I just love pasta to eat,
And sometimes chocolate for a treat.
Pink is a colour I like a lot,
My Peppa Pig is the best present I ever got.
My favourite person is my daddy, who is a gem,
So this, my first poem, is just for them!

Emilia Carlisle (3)
The Beeches Day Nursery, Craigavon

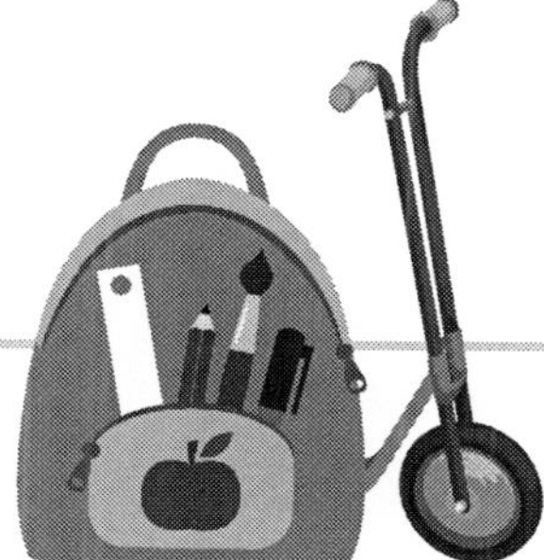

# My First Poem

My name is Ruairi and I go to preschool,
My best friend is Nathan, who is really cool.
I watch Marvel superheroes on TV,
Playing with the small men is lots of fun for me.
I just love chicken goujons to eat,
And sometimes crisps for a treat.
Red is a colour I like a lot,
My green Power Ranger mask is the best present
I ever got.
My favourite person is my brother, Darragh, who is
a gem,
So this, my first poem, is just for them!

Ruairi O'Hagan (4)
The Beeches Day Nursery, Craigavon

# My First Poem

My name is Tami and I go to preschool,
My best friend is Bethany, who is really cool.
I watch Frozen on TV,
Playing duck duck goose is lots of fun for me.
I just love toast to eat,
And sometimes sweets for a treat.
Blue is a colour I like a lot,
My Snow Glow Elsa is the best present I ever got.
My favourite person is Daddy, who is a gem,
So this, my first poem, is just for them!

Tami Catherine Rhysann Surgenor (4)
The Country Preschool, Ballymena

# My First Poem

My name is Bethany and I go to preschool,
My best friend is Tami, who is really cool.
I watch Sleeping Beauty on TV,
Playing with dollies is lots of fun for me.
I just love tomato soup to eat,
And sometimes raspberries and sugar for a treat.
Pink is a colour I like a lot,
My play house is the best present I ever got.
My favourite person is Daddy, who is a gem,
So this, my first poem, is just for them!

Bethany Patterson (4)
The Country Preschool, Ballymena

# My First Poem

My name is Alannah-May and I go to preschool,
My best friend is my sister, Billie-Jo, who is really cool.
I watch PAW Patrol and Dora on TV,
Playing on my scooter is lots of fun for me.
I just love chicken to eat,
And sometimes chocolate for a treat.
Pink is a colour I like a lot,
My Anna doll is the best present I ever got.
My favourite person is my mummy, who is a gem,
So this, my first poem, is just for them!

Alannah-May Kehoe (3)
The Country Preschool, Ballymena

# My First Poem

My name is Sam and I go to preschool,
My best friend is Zain, who is really cool.
I watch Curious George on TV,
Playing with my bus is lots of fun for me.
I just love spaghetti and toast to eat,
And sometimes sweets for a treat.
Red is a colour I like a lot,
My dumper truck is the best present I ever got.
My favourite person is Mummy, who is a gem,
So this, my first poem, is just for them!

Sam McAlonan (4)
The Country Preschool, Ballymena

# My First Poem

My name is Harry and I go to preschool,
My best friend is Alannah-May, who is really cool.
I watch PAW Patrol and Peppa Pig on TV,
Playing with my drum kit is lots of fun for me.
I just love scrambled eggs to eat,
And sometimes sweeties for a treat.
Orange is a colour I like a lot,
My Mario Kart is the best present I ever got.
My favourite person is Annabelle, who is a gem,
So this, my first poem, is just for them!

Harry McNeilly (4)
The Country Preschool, Ballymena

# My First Poem

My name is Nicole and I go to preschool,
My best friend is Emily, who is really cool.
I watch Balamory on TV,
Playing mummies and daddies is lots of fun for me.
I just love chicken and rice to eat,
And sometimes chocolate brownie for a treat.
Purple is a colour I like a lot,
My big girl bed is the best present I ever got.
My favourite person is my big sister, Caitlin, who is a gem,
So this, my first poem, is just for them!

Nicole McKay (4)
The Country Preschool, Ballymena

# My First Poem

My name is Ethan and I go to preschool,
My best friend is Jamie, who is really cool.
I watch Ben 10 on TV,
Playing games is lots of fun for me.
I just love sausage rolls to eat,
And sometimes custard for a treat.
Green is a colour I like a lot,
My Ben 10 is the best present I ever got.
My favourite person is Mummy, who is a gem,
So this, my first poem, is just for them!

Ethan McLaughlin (4)
The Country Preschool, Ballymena

# My First Poem

My name is Robbie and I go to preschool,
My best friend is Matthew, who is really cool.
I watch Fireman Sam on TV,
Playing with my tractors and cow shed is lots of fun for me.
I just love Super Noodles to eat,
And sometimes chocolate for a treat.
Black is a colour I like a lot,
My bin lorry from New York is the best present I ever got.
My favourite person is Daddy, who is a gem,
So this, my first poem, is just for them!

Robbie Gibson (4)
The Country Preschool, Ballymena

# My First Poem

My name is Tom and I go to preschool,
My best friend is Sophie, who is really cool.
I watch cartoons on TV,
Playing with cars is lots of fun for me.
I just love chicken to eat,
And sometimes sweets for a treat.
Green is a colour I like a lot,
My digger is the best present I ever got.
My favourite person is Mummy, who is a gem,
So this, my first poem, is just for them!

Tom Monaghan (4)
The Old School House, Lisburn

# My First Poem

My name is Arianna and I go to preschool,
My best friend is Amelia, who is really cool.
I watch Horrid Henry on TV,
Playing house is lots of fun for me.
I just love pasta to eat,
And sometimes a bun for a treat.
Purple is a colour I like a lot,
My doll is the best present I ever got.
My favourite person is Mummy, who is a gem,
So this, my first poem, is just for them!

Arianna Laughlin (4)
The Old School House, Lisburn

# My First Poem

My name is Riley and I go to preschool,
My best friend is Micah , who is really cool.
I watch Spider-Man on TV,
Playing with Micah is lots of fun for me.
I just love ravioli to eat,
And sometimes getting a toy for a treat.
Black is a colour I like a lot,
My Spider-Man is the best present I ever got.
My favourite person is Daddy, who is a gem,
So this, my first poem, is just for them!

Riley Patrick McGuinness (3)
Willaston Playgroup, Isle Of Man

# My First Poem

My name is Lily and I go to preschool,
My best friend is Ellie, who is really cool.
I watch Toy Story on TV,
Playing and pretending to be cars is lots of fun for me.
I just love crisps to eat,
And sometimes go to town to get sweets for a treat.
Pink is a colour I like a lot,
My story book is the best present I ever got.
My favourite person is Mummy, who is a gem,
So this, my first poem, is just for them!

Lily Davies (4)
Willaston Playgroup, Isle Of Man

# My First Poem

My name is Bobby and I go to preschool,
My best friend is Cody, who is really cool.
I watch The Simpsons on TV,
Playing who can chase who and motorbikes is lots of fun for me.
I just love sandwiches, yoghurt and cake to eat,
And sometimes I go to McDonald's for a treat.
Blue is a colour I like a lot,
My sidecar is the best present I ever got.
My favourite person is my nana, who is a gem,
So this, my first poem, is just for them!

Bobby Edward Kewley (4)
Willaston Playgroup, Isle Of Man

# My First Poem

My name is Cody and I go to preschool,
My best friend is Tyler, who is really cool.
I watch Rescue Bots which I pause and go upstairs for a wee on TV,
Playing with cars is lots of fun for me.
I just love breakfast and toast and Daddy's Frosties to eat,
And sometimes I go to the park for a treat.
Blue is a colour I like a lot,
My Thomas chair is the best present I ever got.
My favourite person is Daddy, who is a gem,
So this, my first poem, is just for them!

Cody Leigh (4)
Willaston Playgroup, Isle Of Man

# My First Poem

My name is Cole and I go to preschool,
My best friend is Dylan, who is really cool.
I watch Toy Story on TV,
Playing Sonic, Iron Man and Batman is lots of fun for me.
I just love chicken nuggets and chips to eat,
And sometimes a pork pie for a treat.
Blue is a colour I like a lot,
My tractor is the best present I ever got.
My favourite person is Mummy, who is a gem,
So this, my first poem, is just for them!

Cole Gregory (3)
Willaston Playgroup, Isle Of Man

# My First Poem

My name is Dylan and I go to preschool,
My best friend is Cole, who is really cool.
I watch Fireman Sam on TV,
Playing Superman is lots of fun for me.
I just love chicken nuggets to eat,
And sometimes I get a breakfast bar for a treat.
Red is a colour I like a lot,
My talking Minions is the best present I ever got.
My favourite person is Mummy, who is a gem,
So this, my first poem, is just for them!

Dylan King (3)
Willaston Playgroup, Isle Of Man

# My First Poem

My name is Jessica and I go to preschool,
My best friend is Ellie, who is really cool.
I watch Frozen on TV,
Playing with my ice castle is lots of fun for me.
I just love carrots to eat,
And sometimes I go to the swings for a treat.
White is a colour I like a lot,
My ice castle is the best present I ever got.
My favourite person is Nana, who is a gem,
So this, my first poem, is just for them!

Jessica Dorothy Hewitt (3)
Willaston Playgroup, Isle Of Man

# My First Poem

My name is Kieran and I go to preschool,
My best friend is Bobby, who is really cool.
I watch Thomas the Tank and Dora the Explorer on TV,
Playing Chinese restaurants is lots of fun for me.
I just love Smiley Faces, waffles, sausages and chicken to eat,
And sometimes sweeties for a treat.
Blue is a colour I like a lot,
My Thomas bed is the best present I ever got.
My favourite person is Billy, who is a gem,
So this, my first poem, is just for them!

Kieran Allan Robert Panter (4)
Willaston Playgroup, Isle Of Man

# My First Poem

My name is Kerry and I go to preschool,
My best friend is Mollie-Mai, who is really cool.
I watch Frozen on TV,
Playing with dolls is lots of fun for me.
I just love yoghurt to eat,
And sometimes I go to Disney on Ice for a treat.
Pink is a colour I like a lot,
My Elsa dress is the best present I ever got.
My favourite person is Mummy, who is a gem,
So this, my first poem, is just for them!

Kerry Chatham (4)
Willaston Playgroup, Isle Of Man

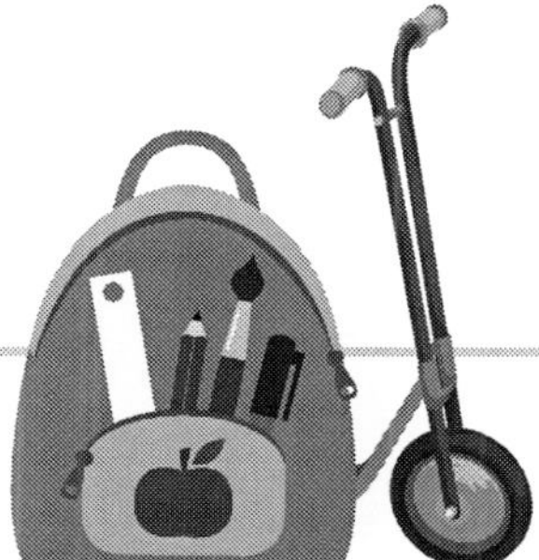

# My First Poem

We hope you have enjoyed reading this book – and that you will continue to enjoy it in the coming years.

If you're a young writer who enjoys reading and creative writing, or the parent of an enthusiastic poet or story writer, do visit our websites, www.myfirstpoem.com and www.youngwriters.co.uk. Here you will find free competitions, workshops and games, as well as recommended reads, a poetry glossary and our blog.

If you would like to order further copies of this book, or any of our other titles, then please give us a call or visit www.myfirstpoem.com.

My First Poem
Remus House
Coltsfoot Drive
Peterborough
PE2 9BF

Tel: 01733 898110
info@myfirstpoem.com